30. AUG. 1989

3029

CHESTER, C.

Going alone

This book is due for return on or before the last date shown above but it may be renewed by personal application, post, or telephone, quoting this date and details of the book.

✿Northamptonshire Leisure and Libraries

GOING ALONE

The Woman's Guide to Travel Know-How

CAROLE CHESTER

CHRISTOPHER HELM
London

© 1987 Carole Chester
Christopher Helm (Publishers) Ltd, Imperial House,
21-25 North Street, Bromley, Kent BR1 1SD

Chester, Carole
    Going alone: the woman's guide to travel
    know-how.
    1. Travel — Handbooks, manuals, etc.
    2. Women travellers — Handbooks, manuals,
    etc.
    I. Title
    910.2'02   G151

ISBN 0-7470-0404-8

Typeset by Leaper & Gard Ltd, Bristol, England
Printed and bound in the Channel Islands by
The Guernsey Press Company Ltd, Guernsey, Channel Islands

CONTENTS

Introduction   vii

Europe
 1. Belgium   3
 2. France   8
 3. Greece   15
 4. Holland   20
 5. Hungary   26
 6. Italy   30
 7. Malta   36
 8. Portugal   40
 9. Romania   44
 10. Scandinavia   48
 11. The Socialist Bloc   54
 12. Spain   58
 13. Switzerland   63
 14. Turkey   67
 15. UK   72
 16. West Germany and Austria   78
 17. Yugoslavia   84

The Middle East
 18. Cyprus   91
 19. Egypt   94
 20. Israel   100

Africa
 21. Morocco and Tunisia   109
 22. Kenya   114

Asia and the Far East
 23. India   121
 24. Japan   127
 25. China   133
 26. Thailand   139
 27. Malaysia   144
 28. Indonesia   148
 29. Australia and New Zealand   153

The Americas
30. Canada 161
31. USA 166
32. Mexico 172
33. Caribbean 177
34. South America 182

Index 193

INTRODUCTION

How many times have you sat in your hotel room in some place far from home, wondering if it's the done thing to walk into the bar alone for a drink ... worrying if it's dangerous to walk around the corner to a café for a sandwich. Or perhaps you're about to decide whether or not you should travel alone. In either case, the following pages will hopefully answer some of your questions and help with that all important decision.

'When are you free to come with me to Ibiza ... Rome ... Mexico — I don't like travelling alone.' Stephanie, a woman of mature years, often says this, but she is a professional travel photographer whose work has taken her around the world. Usually alone. She has found herself in the mountains of Thailand and the temples of India and whilst she may not have liked the idea of being company-less, she has always returned with boundless energy and happy stories. I, too, with some trepidation have found myself in faraway places where my real survival kit was me — and enjoyed it.

Plenty of women, by necessity, must travel alone either on business or on holiday. Plenty more prefer travelling alone because they meet more people that way. There aren't any hard and fast rules about how to do it just as there aren't any guarantees of a great time; but there can be guidance.

Nine times out of ten, almost anywhere in the world, you will be safe hitchhiking, walking at night, taking public transportation. It is the tenth time that causes the worry. Every city has undesirable quarters where a woman alone would not be advised to visit at night. Every country has its own culture and attitudes which may vary from yours and which, if misunderstood, may lead to some sticky situations.

Some destinations are best not considered at all. Africa, for example, is a huge continent, comprising various states and republics with varying degrees of development and 'Westernisation'. Not all of it is as holiday-minded as Kenya and much of it suffers from political unrest. In Nigeria, for example, a *male* friend of mine was mugged whilst walking along the beach in broad daylight by a group of young blacks. After he handed over his watch — the only thing of value he had on him — they proceeded to chase him several miles back to his hotel. And he is a broad shouldered six footer!

This same gentleman was dealt a double dose of ulcers. When visiting his local business office in the early evening, he was almost shot

INTRODUCTION

by a bow and arrow, the weapon carried by the local night watchman, whilst trying to extract his ID card. I am well aware that women can and do visit West African countries such as Nigeria, but it is generally for business purposes in which case they would normally be met and escorted by colleagues residing there. Countries to which I would not send a lady tourist with my blessing are excluded from this guide.

We women of the West have fought hard for our independence and for such formerly male options as lighting up a cigarette in a public place. We've been known (and admired) for wearing mini skirts, hot pants — going topless if we care to. But mode of dress and behaviour differs around the world. Not all societies are as open minded as ours and, in some cases, the 'wrong' dress may lead to a spell in gaol, at the very least an unsolicited 'invitation'. Sometimes even a style of clothing has the wrong effect. I remember wearing a Pucci evening gown to the opening of a new hotel in Tehran (when Iran was still under the Shah's rule). The following evening, elsewhere, I heard one of Queen Farah's relatives remark that only a prostitute would wear clothing with the designer's name written all over it! Nowadays, I suppose, Iranian women aren't seen in anything but the veil — one of the reasons you won't find certain Middle Eastern countries explored in this guide.

I should point out that what you take with you on your travels can be important even though you can buy Schweppes tonic in a Tunisian supermarket, Ambre Solaire in Benidorm, familiar US brands in the UK and familiar UK brands in the USA. But it isn't always so. Some countries don't allow Western imports; some run short; others may simply be unfamiliar with products we regularly use. I suffered an embarrassing experience not so long ago in Moscow by trying to find some tampax. When I mentioned the product, even the Russian interpreter looked puzzled. With a round-the-mulberry-bush explanation from me, she eventually came up with a word for something she said would do and off I trotted to the local equivalent of a chemist. I assumed I was asking for some form of sanitary towel but I wound up with cotton wool — and a red face.

Medical Survival

Such practicalities need to be considered before you travel. A major consideration is the medical question. UK citizens do have the advantage of the National Health System which has a reciprocal agreement with other EEC countries to reduce medical costs. To show you are entitled to these benefits you need an E111 form which may be obtained before you travel from your local Department of Health and Social Security Office. Ask for the leaflet SA28 which explains all the particulars of health services in EEC countries and fill in the form CM1 on the back page.

Don't expect a total refund and it is important to know that no refund is given at all once you are back in the UK. You must expect to pay out in full to the local doctor and/or chemist, get a receipt and show that together with the E111 form to the Social Security office in that country. (Reimbursement varies from country to country.) If hospital treatment is necessary, both hospital and local Social Security Office must be advised you are an insured person holding an E111. Then usually expenses are paid direct although you will still be expected to pay a proportion of the bill.

EEC country or not, medical insurance should be your prime concern. Holiday packages always offer it, often compulsorily. Major insurance companies like Bishopsgate offer comprehensive holiday insurance plans which include medical coverage to a high degree, for a specified length of time (i.e. duration of holiday) or by the year (for the business traveller constantly on the move). Americans shouldn't think of stepping abroad without something similar.

Getting Around on Your Own

If you're travelling independently, shop around for the best buys. Most US airlines, for example, feature a 'Pass' for purchase outside the US, which can cut costs considerably if plans call for more than one American destination. Similarly, there are rail passes for use by British visitors in the US, and the Britrail Pass for use by Americans in the UK. Both Americans and Britons cay buy the Eurail Pass in their own countries of origin for train travel in Europe for specified periods of time, i.e. from 15 days to a three month pass. Unlimited distances may be travelled within the time span. If you're under 26, you're in further luck, since not only Eurail has its own Youth Pass, but there's an Inter-Rail pass and youth reductions available from Transalpino and Eurotrain.

A little advance knowledge — and preparation — can work wonders. I know women are noted for their incredible stamina, adaptability and ingenuity and I have bumped into them travelling alone whatever their age, contentedly enjoying the gardens of Kashmir, the splendours of the Nile and the magic of the Amazon. The majority of them having an amazing time. I know there are 18-year-old backpackers who trek off to the wilds of Chile or Peru, their only thought, one of excitement. That there are 60-year-olds planning to conquer the Himalayas. All without any help from me. But a few warnings and awareness can make travel that much easier.

In writing *Going Alone* I am not trying to be sexist, but women are 'women people' with differing travel needs and knowledge from men. I trust the following chapters will prove an informative destination guide with YOU specifically in mind.

EUROPE

Of all the regions in the world, Europe is by far the easiest to get around. Given its countries' own differences, its outlook is easier understood, its food more familiar, its peoples' heritage intertwined.

Women have travelled alone through Europe for decades and enjoyed doing so. In the subsequent chapters, we have picked out the most popular countries to be visited together with some of their high — and low — lights.

1 BELGIUM

Only one-fifth the size of Great Britain, Belgium is used to single woman travellers to the point of ignoring them. It is, after all, a centre for commerce not to mention EEC headquarters so it sees a multitude of business executives passing through or residing for a year or two. The hotels and restaurants in Brussels especially are geared to expense account holders and there are no restrictions to bother women.

The country's biggest problem is the political and temperamental difference between the Flemish in the north and the Walloons in the south. Whilst this may affect business negotiations, it will not unsettle the tourist. Rivalry between the two has led to continual parliamentary debate over regional governments, but as it is, the country's central government is in Brussels whilst Walloon and Flemish areas have their own local governments.

The Male Attitude

The Flemish Belgian tends to be somewhat phlegmatic, and rather more rigid and conservative than his French-speaking Walloon 'brother' whose outlook is easier-going. So far as language goes, however, there are no worries since the majority of Belgians speak English, Dutch and German besides their own dialects.

Whilst Belgians as a whole lack the French flair for dress and style, they're less abrasive and more willing to help a foreigner in need than their French neighbours. A Belgian might not exude charm or be adept at flattering, but he is practical. A business or social invitation, by the way, even from a couple, generally means a restaurant meal not a home-cooked one.

Where to Stay

Whether you choose to stay at a pension or a luxury hotel (Belgium has both plus all the inbetweens), you won't encounter difficulties as a woman alone. Most of the better hotels are located in Brussels and are reliant on a business clientele. You'll find top chain names such as Hilton, Sheraton, Ramada and Hyatt with a full range of facilities.

Accommodation in small towns and seaside ports is often family-run and, if it's small, may be called an *auberge, hostellerie* or *gasthof*. Select one recognised by the Belgian authorities — with a sign outside saying so, and with posted rates.

Getting Around on Your Own

Belgium's road network is one of the most dense in Europe — motorways cover much of the country, except for the Ardennes region. All the major car rental companies have offices here so driving is one good way of getting around. Town speeds are 60km an hour; outside, 90 km; and on motorways, 120 km.

Because the Belgians are avid cyclists, many roads have special bike lanes. Since inter-city distances aren't great, cycle rental is an excellent low-priced form of transport. Bikes can be rented by the day or more, without deposit, from a number of train stations and, if you show a train ticket, you'll get a discount.

The train network is reliable, safe and one of Europe's most extensive, providing A1 service for first or second class travel. Basic train fares aren't cheap but there are money saving tickets such as the 'Runabouts' which can be used over five, 10 or 15 consecutive days for travel anywhere on the network. Another 'Runabout' ticket covers any five day travel within a 14-day period. There are day-return tickets or you can buy booklets or reduced-cost, open-dated tickets for day returns during the summer.

Brussels' tram and bus system is a good one and the city also has a modern metro. All public transport is flat fee, which covers transfers from one system to another for a single journey. A tourist's pass for a day's use of the city transport is another idea for getting around.

Belgian taxis are expensive but dependable. Metered prices include taxes and tips but you're best off phoning for one rather than looking for one in the street.

Eating and Drinking Solo

The Belgian penchant for both quality and quantity of food means you'd be a fool merely to stay in your hotel and order room service. The food-conscious Belgians ensure there's no shortage of *charcuteries* and chocolate shops, bistros and watering holes, and they'll linger (alone or not) over a meal even at lunchtime. One of the most 'people' places in Brussels is the restaurant-lined rue de Bouchers whilst the area just north of Grand' Place, known as 'Sacred Isle', is highly recommended as an upper crust locale. You'll find loads of waffle and *frites* stands scattered throughout the city, but skip the small eating places around the Gare du Midi (an area not known for its hygiene).

Most bars serve food of some kind, from light snacks to full meals and there are plenty of indoor and outdoor cafés throughout Belgium. Regional cuisine is distinctive but for almost all of it, beer is a prime ingredient. The variety of beers is extensive, with differently-shaped glasses used for them, but *Artois* is the most universally known.

Belgium is not exactly noted for its highlife, though Brussels has its hotspots and the coastal ports with their casinos (e.g. Ostend) are high spirited in summer, and so full of Britons you'll think it's home-from-home.

The Safety Factor

Belgium is really a very safe country for the female traveller. The emergency number in Brussels for police, fire or ambulance is 900.

No-no's

Don't hitch on main road arteries — it's illegal.
Don't stay in a room near a railway station, like Antwerp's, or you may be taken for a local prostitute.

Essentials

Anything you might want you can find in Belgium's shops, though you may have to pay dearly for it. Friday night is often a late night shopping day and supermarkets at the ports stay open all week. In Brussels the main shopping areas are Boulevard Adolphe Max (downtown), rue Neuve, rue du Marche aux Herbes, rue de l'Ecuyer — and uptown, the rue de Namur, Chaussee d'Ixelles, Avenue de la Toison d'Or and Avenue Louise. Electricity is 220v, 50 cycles.

Medical Survival

Your hotel concierge will direct you to the nearest chemist open at night or on a weekend, or you can find out in Brussels by calling 497 18 18. In a medical emergency, dial 906.

Belgium is an EEC country so British visitors can receive similar benefits to their own National Health Service, providing they hold an E111 form (see Introduction).

What to do Solo

There is more to Belgium than meets the eye, with nine provinces to choose from — but there are only a handful of focal centres of which *Brussels* is the biggest draw.

Brussels is a city of elegant squares such as Place Royal or Place du Petit Sablon. It is also a city of museums: the Kolen is famous for its primitive collection and the Royal Museum of Art and History is one of Europe's largest. One way of spending an interesting morning is to take a look at the flea market in the Place du Jeu de Balle or go to the Grand' Sablon's weekend market.

The capital's Grand' Place is as central as you can get, fine to walk around, either during the day when the flower sellers are out in force, or at night when its old guild halls are illuminated. The main building is the fifteenth-century Town Hall with its tapestries and ornaments, but also look at the Brewers' House, now a museum. The old Bread Market, the 'Maison du Roi', today is also a museum, housing among other things all the uniforms that most famous Brussels monument, 'Manneken Pis', wears. This small bronze statue (Belgium's best known and loved) stands in the rue de l'Etuve, symbolising the somewhat irreverent spirit of the city's inhabitants.

Belgium's most popular tourist centre is *Bruges* on the West Flanders coast and is easily reachable from Ostend. It's a perfectly preserved medieval city, compact enough to walk around if you start at the main square bordered by innumerable cafés. Tucked into narrow side streets, there are fascinating small speciality food shops selling cheese, delicatessen meats and chocolates filled with fresh cream. Bruges boasts many fine and ancient buildings, of course, but in my opinion the top attraction is the Begijnhof convent. Mirror-like canals are another feature.

Ghent is another medieval gem where fifteenth- to seventeenth-century guild houses line the Graslei, a street which, together with the Koornlei across the way, once formed the town's old harbour. Armed with a map, head for St Michael's Bridge for one of the best views of the town. Two notable museums are: Voor Schone Kunsten in Citadel Park (for fine arts) and Museum van Oudheden in Van de Bijlike Abbey (for local history, guild hall and monastery rooms). Many cafés and discos are situated near the University, but for cultural entertainment, bear in mind the Flanders Festival is an annual event from August to September.

Most of *Antwerp's* main sights are concentrated in the old part of town and can easily be seen on a self-guided walking tour. Its museums are a big attraction but many are closed on a Monday. Rubens' House is one — where Rubens lived and worked for 30 years; the Plantin-Moretus, another, housing Plantin's printing tools and presses; the Royal Gallery of Fine Arts is a third recommendation. On weekends, diamond cutting demonstrations are given at the Veiligheidsmuseum. The majority of Antwerp's nightspots are located around the Grote Markt but there are few suitable bars.

Visas and Inoculations

Visas — none required.
Inoculations — none required.

 **Useful Addresses**

Embassies
British Embassy, Britannia House, rue Joseph 11 No. 28, 1040 Brussels. Tel: 217 90 00
US Embassy, Boulevard du Regent 27, 1000 Brussels. Tel: 513 44 50

Tourist Offices
Belgium National Tourist Office, 38 Dover Street, London W1. Tel: 01 499 5379
Belgian Tourist Office, 745 5th Avenue, New York, NY 10015. Tel: (212) 758 8130

2 FRANCE

The French are highly individualistic and, since their country comprises 22 regions divided into 95 *départements* even before the individualism shows itself, it is not surprising that ideas and outlooks are so variable. Views which are acceptable in cosmopolitan, 'wickedly' naughty Paris may not be echoed in the provinces. Anything may go in the south of France, too, but this is hardly so in a region like the Dordogne.

French women traditionally possess chic; Frenchmen, style (at least in any metropolis). Both are independent and argumentative by nature. Partnerless visitors are expected to prove their independence before they're accepted, but the French would be the last to reprove unconventionality.

For a country its size, the contrasts of French climate and terrain are remarkable and its touristic offerings countless. A woman may find it exasperating, but at the height of her exasperation, still rewarding.

The Male Attitude

The French aren't always very helpful and can be downright cantankerous, expecting a foreigner to speak their language, giving no lavish praise to unworthy attempts. However, they can also be exceptionally tolerant, judging strangers for their merit as humans more than anything else. They may not meet a tourist's demands with good grace, but they do meet them albeit reserving their private thoughts with a sigh of regret or mystification.

Underneath a devil-may-care gloss, the average Frenchman holds family life in high regard. He is also proud of who he is and what he is, a national trait that disallows his becoming a brash inconsiderate escort. He may be vain but he is also a charming, attentive companion prone to romantic gestures. He respects and responds to anyone with style and panache.

The French can be very self contained and not make the first move towards conversation with a stranger. They are also averse to criticism of any kind, especially that offered out of ignorance.

Where to Stay

There are no hard and fast rules about which kind of accommodation is best for the single woman, nor even which areas are most suitable. Many one star establishments are perfectly proper, family-run, clean and adequate. Paris, for example, boasts countless good budget pensions in addition to the flea bag variety and the only real way of sorting the wheat from the chaff is by word of mouth recommendation.

Outside Paris you can at least select one of the *Logis* or *Auberges Rurales* to ensure suitability without suffering economic disaster. The *Logis* (several thousand of them) are often situated in the prettiest parts of France and are assisted by government aid to ensure that rooms and facilities are of a good standard and that meals are not skimpy. The *Auberges* are similar but generally more simple, in village locations.

At the other end of the scale, visitors to France will find magnificent hotels like the George Cinq, Meurice or Crillon (all in Paris) or any of the Relais et Châteaux hotels. The latter, situated throughout France (and elsewhere in the world) pride themselves on cuisine, comfort and ambience and may well have formerly been private palaces or villas. Not quite so costly are those members of a consortium known as Relais du Silence, country châteaux in peaceful surroundings.

These days finding a motel is easy enough, in all regions too. Usually they are accessible but a little way from main routes. Self-catering accommodation is well organised through the *Gîte* system, an organisation which lists farm houses, rural houses, furnished flats, etc. which have all met an approved standard and may be rented by the week or season. *Gîtes* may not be the ideal answer for a woman who might consider their out-of-the-way locations too isolated and lonely.

Budget travellers might rather choose to camp — France has some 4,000 registered sites in several grades, including luxury. Camping outside of marked sites, in public countryside or on private property, is not allowed without permission from those concerned and may result in heavy fines.

Making on-the-spot bookings for accommodation can be done through any Syndicat d'Initiative or Acceuil de France office.

Getting Around on Your Own

Hiring a car is easy (or you could take your own) and is perhaps the best way for exploring the more rural regions of France at your own pace, without the worries of keeping to bus or train timetables. Within France, holiday routes are actually signposted with yellow and green arrows to show scenic uncongested routes. Speed limits are strictly enforced — on-the-spot police fines if you drive faster than you should.

French road speeds are complicated. In dry road conditions: 130 km per hour on toll-free motorways; 110 km on dual carriageways; 90 km on other roads; and 60 km in towns (all unless otherwise posted). There is an 80 km per hour minimum on motorways if visibility/conditions are good. In wet road conditions: 110 km per hour on motorways; 100 km for dual carriageways; 80 km on other roads.

To reach a specific destination, the train may serve you better. French rail service is first class, able to boast some of the world's fastest trains. Trans-Europ Expresses, for example, link major towns, travelling at high speed, but these are first class only with advance booking requirements. Other expresses have two classes of seating and almost all long-distance trains have a dining car.

Many reduced fares exist including the France-Vacances rover tickets which allow unlimited travel throughout the network for specified periods of time at a fixed price.

Don't expect long distance coach service. It doesn't exist beyond the tourist excursion or package holdiay variety, or the occasional route such as Paris-Nice. A regular bus service, however, connects all villages and hamlets not rail-linked, and is operated by the French Railways.

Cycling by the way is a national pastime and you'll find special cycle tracks on some routes. Bikes may be rented from shops in almost every town and certainly at railway stations in resort areas.

Getting around Paris by yourself can be fun on foot, bus or metro but driving around this sprawling metropolis is not recommended. Buses show their destinations at front and back, plus their principal stops along the side. The metro is surprisingly easy and safe to use (though watch out for pickpockets) but it does close down at 1 a.m. (disco goers take heed). A tourist book or *carnet* of tickets may be purchased at metro stations for use on metro or buses. Taxis are plentiful but won't always stop when signalled if there's a rank close by. They are metered but that doesn't mean no rip-offs! Walkers around central Paris should keep an eye out for light-fingered gypsies, often in family packs. They're not dangerous but they will lighten your pockets.

 ## Eating and Drinking Solo

Tourist restaurants (with a fixed price menu), brasseries, cafés and bistros are the most comfortable places to eat and drink solo. Cafés, from the plush sidewalk type so ubiquitous in Paris or Nice to the tin pot variety in the smallest village, are an integral part of French life. They are used to patrons lingering for hours over a coffee or *kir* whether or not they order food. In cities like Paris, self-service bars, fast food outlets (including McDonald's) plus crêperies are a thought. In the countryside, look for a *relais routiers* sign for good food at reasonable prices.

Don't think twice about venturing into any café/bar — nobody else does. Jazz and rock clubs of all descriptions can be found along the Seine in Paris between rue St Jacques and rue Bonaparte. The big nightspots with lavish revues are so large that a lone woman won't stick out like a sore thumb (e.g. the Lido or Folies Bergère) nor will you be barred from any discothèque, unless for membership reasons.

The range of French food and wines defies description, let it just be said that numerous regional specialities can be sampled. Of special interest in Normandy and Brittany are shellfish, Calvados (apple brandy) and crêpes; unusual northern French dishes include rabbit with prunes; the Loire is particularly noted for its wines; the Dordogne for pâtés and liquor-soaked fruits.

The Safety Factor

Providing good sense is maintained, France on your own is pretty safe. An unescorted late night stroll by the Seine is not advised, nor indeed in any deserted part of the city. Hitching on country lanes or camping alone in forested regions far from the crowds has its charm, but also its risk factor.

No-no's

Don't get embroiled in a political conversation. Bear in mind there is strong resentment towards the centralised French government in the southwest of the country where a Spanish influence prevails.
Don't hitchhike on motorways — it's illegal.
Don't forget to tip — everyone from the public toilet attendants to the film theatre usherettes.
Skip the hotels in the Place de la Contrescarpe area of Paris — there are too many sleazy ones.
Don't expect all French beaches to accept topless or nude sunbathing — they're not all the Côte d'Azur.
Don't think badly of French ports.

Essentials

French city shops stock everything but opening and closing hours vary regionally, so don't leave the purchase of necessities until the last moment. Fashions and perfumes are natural buys especially in Paris and Nice. Outside large towns, look for a hypermarket (some of which open Sunday) selling many goods including food.
Electricity is 220v, 50 cycles.

Medical Survival

Pharmacies sell medicines, first aid items and toiletries. Most of them are independently owned and will happily recommend products for minor ills. They can be spotted by a green cross above the door, lit during opening hours. A hotel concierge will always help you to get an English-speaking doctor or you can call the nearest Commisariat de Police.

In Paris, the Pharmacie Dhery on the Champs Elysées is open 24 hours (tel: 256 02 41). For the city's 24-hour doctor service, tel: 242 37 00 or 337 77 77.

British visitors carrying an E111 form (see Introduction) can obtain partial reimbursement for outlays in France if medical attention is required or hospital treatment is necessary.

Unless it says otherwise tap water is safe to drink. Nevertheless, the French themselves all consume bottled water which is very good and not expensive.

What to do Solo

First get your bearings in *Paris*, by organised coach or boat excursion or from a high vantage point. From the top of Notre Dame's south tower you can look over the heart of Paris; from the Arc de Triomphe, the Bois de Boulogne; and from the Tour Eiffel, the whole of Paris is at your feet. A trip on a Bâteaux Mouches down the Seine will point out the sights and save your feet. The boats operate frequent excursions from several bridges.

The most significant areas in the capital are: the Opéra Quarter where you'll find smart shops and grandiose architecture including the famous Opéra House itself and the Madelaine. Famous department stores, Printemps and Galeries Lafayette plus those shopping streets with ultra chic — rue du Faubourg St-Honoré and rue de la Paix — are all within the quarter. Pop concerts are often held in the Olympia auditorium. American visitors are likely to be found in Harry's Bar on rue Daunou.

Les Halles is still in transition from what was a market to what may be a lively shopping and entertainment district. Some of it is rather seedy but the Pompidou Centre is worth looking in at, for those interested in art and design. Le Marais, also an old district, is far gentler since its restoration and boasts many fine museums amid its rambling streets.

The Latin Quarter is the heart of the Left Bank, notable for colourful cafés, bookshops and students. Former Bohemian Montparnasse has been rather torn apart by redevelopment but its Right Bank counterpart, Montmartre, has struggled to retain its character. Pigalle is sleazy and tawdry and the atmosphere around the Sacré Coeur, rather too touristy. Some fascinating mementoes of the district in its artistic heyday are to be seen, however, in the Musée de Montmartre on rue St Vincent.

Ile de la Cité is the historic nub of Paris where Notre Dame stands. Its adjacent district, Ile St-Louis is more private, more picturesque. Only pockets of history are visible in the quarter of St Germain but its three great cafes — Flore, Lipp and Deux Magots — are where half the world meets the other half.

There are no restrictions for women in Paris and an infinite, wonderful collection of landmark buildings and museums can be seen. To find out about current events or seasonal shows, buy 'Pariscope' or 'Officiel des Spectacles' (listing lectures and guided tours besides). 'Paris City' is the monthly publication for foreigners.

Normandy and *Brittany* are popular provinces for beach lovers who can use resorts, like Deauville, Trouville or St Malo, as a holiday base. The *Loire Valley* and *Dordogne* are attractive regions for the motorist who likes country scenes and castles. Strasbourg is an admirable base for exploring Alsace and its wine country and Dijon, for exploring *Burgundy*. River and canal cruises on the Rivers Loire, Dordogne and Rhône are a possibility for those tired of their own company. Riding holidays may be the answer for the active single; a sojourn at a health spa for the more restful.

To see and be seen, go to the Riviera where *Nice* is the prime centre. Promenade des Anglais borders those celebrated pebbled beaches and overpriced cafés border it. There are public and private beaches where beach attire (if and when worn) is as ritzy as the boutiques along rue Massena. (Watering spots here are best for early evening aperitifs and people-gazing.) For better beaches you need to travel to Beaulieu, Villefranche-sur-Mer or Cap d'Ail.

If you can afford it, *Cannes* is another wealthy Riviera base with its luxury establishments on La Croisette and its fancy shops along rue d'Antibes. There is a charge to use La Croisette's beach strip, but not the public ones west of the port. At glamorous *St Tropez* private clubs flank the area around Plage de Tahiti but the best public beach is Plage des Salins. The whole of the French Riviera is so well known, it's a good place for singles of both sexes — it certainly attracts enough of them.

Visas and Inoculations

Visa — none required.
Inoculations — none required.

Useful Addresses

Embassies
British Embassy, 109 rue du Faubourg St-Honoré, 75008 Paris. Tel: 42 66 91 42
US Embassy, 2 Avenue Gabriel, 75382 Paris. Tel: 42 96 12 02

FRANCE

Tourist Offices and Hotel Chains
Paris Tourist Office, 127 Avenue des Champs-Elysées, Paris.
Tel: 723 61 72
French Government Tourist Office, 178 Piccadilly, London W1.
Tel: 01 491 7622
French Tourist Office, 610 Fifth Avenue, New York, NY 10020.
Tel: (212) 575 1125
Relais & Châteaux Hotels, 10 Place de la Concorde, Paris.
Tel: 47 42 00

3 GREECE

Greece may put on a modern face but underneath it loves the traditional. Most of the population are Greek Orthodox and that means pretty strict rules which have to be observed. Traditions are exemplified by the fact that even today elderly (and some quite young) women dress in black — particularly in the more isolated villages — and that men are often to be seen around taverna tables seemingly doing little else but discussing politics.

Politics have always played a big part in Greece but unless your knowledge of the subject and your language is of university level, it's best not to get involved. It is perhaps not the best time either to discuss your Turkish friends; and please don't mistake a mainland Greek for a Greek Cypriot if you wish to make a good impression.

The Male Attitude

On the surface Greeks readily accept the sole woman with a mind and a style of her own. Scratch below the surface, however, and there may be a different attitude for the average Greek male is still having trouble getting used to independent women. At heart, he is a family man, more than likely the apple of his mother's eye, and one with a typical Mediterranean temperament, expecting a woman to be at his beck and call.

The attitude can lead to misinterpretations for whilst Athenians are reasonably worldly wise (being big city dwellers) fishermen in small villages could well think a lone female signifies invitation to pester. There are no restrictions for entering nightspots but be prepared to be solicited. One of the reasons is that Greek men have become used to the influx of North European women looking for sex and, therefore, can't always differentiate between those and others who merely wish to dance or listen to the music. One good thing is that most Greeks won't push their luck too far and will take a firm 'no' for an answer.

The tolerant overlay on the traditional is evident in the attitude to topless bathing. It is illegal and can result in a trip to prison, but that doesn't mean you won't find it. Usually, these beaches (mostly on the islands) are away from the family ones. A woman should suss out the areas before taking everything off! (One of the famous — or infamous if you like — cases of a turned blind eye is nude Paradise Beach on Mykonos and the nearby gay male nude beach, Super Paradise.)

Where to Stay

The Athens cosmopolitan hotels are used to caring for and feeding the single traveller but their bars do tend to be favoured by prostitutes. A businesswoman might well look for accommodation in a hotel of the Grande Bretagne ilk — especially protective of its guests.

Lesser hotels vary considerably: Athens has innumerable cheap hotels but many are on the sleazy side, like the dives by the station. In mainland and island resort areas there are both luxury hotels and very simple (but adequate) accommodation. Taverna and pension rooms in Greece tend to be basic but are perfectly recommendable. Often, they are family-run and if you make friends with the owners, you'll be particularly welcomed. On the islands it is possible literally to knock on doors seeking lodging.

Getting Around on Your Own

Not that easy what with Cyrillic signs, and public transport that may well depart late or not at all. There are vast differences in mainland terrain and on many islands some places are only accessible by small boat. A train service connects the main cities and there is a more extensive network of bus routes. Local city and town buses need a firm flagging down or they may whizz straight past. Taxis are plentiful but so popular they are hard to get. Athens has a subway system and rental cars are readily available although city driving is frenzied. On the other hand, a car is really necessary to explore much of the Greek mainland properly.

From Piraeus, there is a regular ferry service to most of the Aegean islands, but watch out if making inter-island connections. This is where it becomes confusing and unreliable. The frequency of inter-island services seems to vary almost according to whim. Some islands have a daily shuttle service, some weekly, but hardly any stick to written schedules. And the small passenger boats arrive and depart in a flash — if you're not there waiting, you'll literally miss the boat! The sea, too, can whip up at a moment's notice and you may well get stranded on an island. If you're not travelling on a package holiday, you can never check and recheck enough.

Once on an island, getting around alone should be relatively simple. You can expect to find some sort of local bus service but the best and most economical way is by rented bike or moped. Small boat rental can often be negotiated.

Eating and Drinking Solo

Skip the ports and there's no real problem with dining or drinking alone in any of the tourist spots. Most of the cafés and tavernas are outdoors anyway, with no feeling of being bottled up and a very informal atmosphere. Don't worry about being unable to read the menu — it's the done thing in the small places to head for the kitchen and make a visual selection. Simple dishes are inexpensive but don't expect food to arrive at the table piping hot. Still, in the sunshine it doesn't seem to matter. When you're looking for company (or crowds) dine late — the Greeks do. If you don't fancy a restaurant, look for food stalls selling *souvlaki* (grilled meat on sticks) and *tiropita* (small pastry triangles containing cheese).

Ouzo, the national drink, is very cheap and is quite pleasant mixed with lemonade (as an alternative to water). Greek wines are hardly *appellation contrôlée* but there are many available varieties of the local grape. *Retsina* is the best known of all and you can buy it in small bottles (icy cold) from any taverna. Greek coffee (like Turkish) is dark and syrupy; the café alternative is invariably Nescafé but regular brewed coffee is available in the large hotels.

The Safety Factor

Providing you use good common sense, Greece is as safe a country as any for the woman alone. The two organisations which handle tourism handle it well: the GNTO (National Tourist Organisation of Greece) which gives all the general information about accommodation and sights throughout the mainland and islands, and the Touristiki Astinomia or Tourist Police who deal with any local problem which might arise. Don't be afraid to ask them to find you a room, a doctor or what to do if your wallet is stolen. In Athens dial 171 for the Tourist Police, 100 for emergency police.

No-no's

Don't hitch along any roads other than main ones and even then it may be bothersome.
Don't walk along port areas alone at night.
Be prepared to cover your shoulders when visiting churches and monasteries and don't wear short-shorts.
Check out a beach before going topless.

Essentials

Greece and her islands can be extremely hot during the summer months so cotton clothing is the most comfortable. High humidity prevents quick drying so don't be stingy with lingerie or beach wear. Take high-protection sun creams for island lazing and a sun hat for sightseeing.

Major city and island capital shops are well stocked with necessary toiletries but small islands like Paxos (which at last check didn't even have a hairdresser) will only have limited items available.

Electricity is 220v, 50 cycles in Athens and most of the mainland, 110v elsewhere.

Medical Survival

Imported pharmaceuticals are available. Bottled water is advisable anywhere outside Athens or large resorts. Since Greece is a member of the EEC, there is a reciprocal arrangement with the British NHS. The Tourist Police or hotel will help to locate an English-speaking doctor and for medical emergencies in Athens tel: 166.

What to do Solo

Athens' archaeological sites are its key attraction and there are plenty of them to keep a lone traveller busy. The Acropolis is the city's crowning point where, in spite of the passing of hundreds of years, its four buildings are a reminder of ancient Greek glories: the Parthenon, Temple of Athena Nike, the Propylae and the Erechtheum. The best preserved Greek temple is that of Hephaistos whose Agora contains the ruins of the city's old administrative centre. And for splendid bronzes, look in at the National Archaeological Museum.

Focal point for people-watching is Syntagma Square, bordered by pricey 'tourist' cafés. Between here and the Acropolis lies the Plaka, a lively touristy area for shopping and nightlife. To reach the flea market at Monastiraki, take Ermous Street from Syntagma; by way of contrast, the Kolonaki district (about five minutes away) is considered a 'posh' area. Athens' other big (and noisy) square is Omonia, the heart of downtown, but you'll need a taxi or the subway to reach the port of Piraeus where you're best off with an escort. Athens' own resort area is the Glyfada coast where there are holiday hotels, cafés and nightspots — and topless sunning is okay for women.

There are so many Greek islands that choosing one is like asking a sweet-toothed friend to pick between cherry cheesecake and chocolate gâteau. It is safe to say that the smaller the island, the more comfortable you may feel since faces soon become familiar. The smaller the island, of course, the less things there are to do — not an incentive for the very active.

Among the larger most popular islands, *Corfu* has a high rating with British visitors. You'll need wheels of some kind to get around and will be hard put to find a sandy beach, but it's very busy and jammed with accommodation of all kinds, including single people's favourite, Club Med. A favourite holiday centre on *Rhodes* is Lindos, crowned by an acropolis reached by foot or on donkey. Its maze of cobbled alleyways are lined with tiny shops, cafés and pension rooms, all crowded in summer. In *Crete*, tourists have a preference for Agios Nikolaos and *the* sightseeing excursion is to Knossos.

Visas and Inoculations

Visa — none required.
Inoculations — none required.

Useful Addresses

Embassies
British Embassy, 1 Ploutarchou Street, Athens 10675. Tel: 723 6211
US Embassy, 91 Vasse. Sophias Blvd, Athens 10160. Tel: 721 2951

Tourist Offices
Greek National Tourist Office, 195/197 Regent Street, London W1. Tel: 01 734 5997
Greek Tourist Office, Olympic Tower, 645 Fifth Avenue, New York, NY 10022. Tel: (212) 421 5777

4 HOLLAND

At the crossroads of Europe, Holland — or The Netherlands — however one refers to it, is one of the easiest countries for a woman to visit and enjoy being alone in. It is small, neat and compact and the Dutch themselves are a well mannered, tolerant people with a similar outlook to the British. Holland is a well organised country too with excellent tourist facilities, so that anyone in trouble or needing information will find aid easily and quickly.

Like most small countries these days, Holland (which prospered on trade during the Middle Ages) needs tourists for her economy, but hospitality is part of the Dutch nature and as warm a welcome will be found in Amsterdam, the capital, as in the little villages. A policy of 'live and let live' attracted rather too many hippies in the past, but that same benevolence allows residents and visitors to be as individual as they care to be.

At the peak of Dutch colonialism, many officials and planters married Indonesian women and brought them home to Holland. This was the beginning of what is today a fairly large Indonesian community. Although in recent years there has been some racial conflict, for the most part the 'East' and 'West' live together in harmony.

The Male Attitude

In Holland, there is scarcely a difference between a 'male' attitude and a 'female' one. Both sexes have a good sense of humour and an easy-going outlook. You'll find that out if you indulge in Amsterdam nightlife which runs the gamut of 'anything goes' — from topless lady bands to gay clubs and discothèques where the air is obviously thick with 'pot'.

Almost by way of contrast, the Dutch generally have a good solid approach to family life, are traditional and love to keep up old customs.

The Dutch businessman is kind, courteous and charming. Any local man bumped into in one of the cafés (*the* social centres of Holland) will be interested, conversational and friendly without being pushy. Most of the Dutch — certainly the younger ones — speak English well so no one need fear a language problem as can happen in other parts of Europe. You can feel comfortable about accepting an invitation for a drink or a dance without feeling there's going to be a fight for your honour at the end of it.

Where to Stay

However modest, Dutch hotels and guest houses are among the cleanest and most comfortable in Europe, and efficiency is a national trademark. Rates often include a hearty version of continental breakfast with additions of cheese and ham so there's real value for money. Large chains with UK and US offices, like the Hilton, run properties in Amsterdam and Rotterdam whilst Golden Tulip Hotels are linked to KLM. A full list of accommodation is available from the Netherlands National Tourist Office in London, New York or any of its information offices (known as VVV) in Holland.

Should you arrive without a reservation, the VVV Logies Informatie Dienst (Accommodation Service) will find you a room. This nationwide hotel reservation system is run by the tourist office for a small fee, but you must turn up in person.

Getting Around on Your Own

Driving is one hassle-free way of getting around. Thanks to a first class road network and the easy availability of car hire, you can consider this mode of transport without worry. All you need is a passport, valid driving licence and be 21 or over. Dutch roads are classified by the European numbering system and, unless otherwise shown, there is no speed limit on open highways — only in cities and built-up areas when it is usually 50 km an hour. When driving in the Netherlands, remember that trams have priority and watch out for the cyclists — cycling's not only a mode of transport but a national pastime. The only drawback to hiring a car is city parking. In Amsterdam, particularly, what with its canals and one-ways, finding a parking spot can be frustrating.

Renting a bike may be a worthwhile alternative. Bikes can be hired inexpensively by the hour, day or for longer at reduced rates — from hotels or from almost 90 railway stations including those in all the major cities. All that is required is some kind of identification and a deposit.

Because of the popularity of biking, Holland provides specific cycle tracks marked by a round blue sign with a white bike symbol on it. When they do exist, they must be used by all moped and bike riders. In summer, by the way, the Netherlands Railway runs special night bicycle trains between the large cities and holiday areas. Information on touring routes is available at any of the VVV offices.

Trains are comfortable, dependable and safe for the solo female, offering frequent efficient service between destinations. They do run to schedule and all the main cities are linked by non-stop, inter-city trains. You can obtain timetables from railway stations, bookstalls and newspaper kiosks. Tourist tickets are a good bet if you intend to travel extensively but there are also cheap-day returns.

Those on a low budget might think about the inter-city coach service for getting around. Various bus companies offer cheap-day returns or you can also buy strip tickets (from bus or tram drivers, bus ticket offices and sometimes VVV offices) at a reduced rate, good for rides anywhere in the country. In addition to buses and trams, Amsterdam and Rotterdam also have metro systems and all fares are zone based.

In the cities you are not likely to be ripped off if you take a taxi. They're metered and besides, it is not a Dutch habit to overcharge. However, finding a cruising taxi isn't easy. Generally, they are found at a rank or phoned for. The price on the meter includes tax and tip and for travel outside cities or between cities, there are fixed rates.

Boat travel is another good way of seeing Holland. After all, there are over 1,000 lakes here and innumerable canals. Favourite sight-seeing trips include those around Rotterdam's harbour and those glass-topped canal boats in Amsterdam. Passenger boat services operate to the Wadden and Frisian Islands.

Eating and Drinking Solo

No shortage of places; no problems. Taverns or wine and cheese cellars are ideally suited to singles and are especially prevalent in Amsterdam. The dark wood panelled cosy cafés in the Jordaan area are really pleasant retreats and there are all kinds of open-air cafés wherever you go. Those along the canals are lively and atmospheric, whilst those in Leidesplein may not be so charming but are always busy and loud with music.

If you're looking for a snack meal on your own, go to one of the *broodjeswinkels* (sandwich shops) where you can purchase soft buns with a wide choice of fillings, all at low prices. You may also buy food from kerbside stalls — fresh herring in season, perhaps — without worrying about subsequent tummy trouble since hygiene is very much a matter of Dutch fact.

Nightspots do tend to charge an entrance fee and you may get the once-over before being allowed in. Skip the sailors' quarter of Amsterdam — Nieuwendijk-Zeedijk, but Thorbeckeplein, Rembrandt-splein and Leidesplein are all good, safe, areas for nightlife, with plenty of bars, beat music and discos. In summer, the seaside resorts of Scheveningen, Zandvoort and Noordwijk have a lot going on, but otherwise don't expect a blaze of neon in Holland's small towns.

Happily, Holland's bars tend to be the convivial variety attracting a young crowd. You can expect to meet both locals and tourists in any of them and needn't be afraid of asking for a *genever* gin — no one's going to look askance. Don't be surprised if a stranger asks where you're from or how you're enjoying yourself.

The Dutch love to eat and drink and restaurants suit all budgets.

Do try an Indonesian *rijstafel* at least once, and expect to find cheese served in a variety of ways. *Pils* and *Amstel* are two of Holland's best beers, but if you've a sweet tooth try one of the many liqueurs that have been produced since the seventeenth century. The choice in any *bodega* is large, the price is low. *Genever* is the national drink, more viscous and sweet than those you may be used to and normally drunk well chilled, without a mixer. *Jonge* (young) *genever* contains less sugar than *oude* (old) whilst fruit gins like *bessenjenever* (redcurrant) or *citroenjenever* (lemon) are both known as ladies' gins!

The Safety Factor

Providing one uses common sense and discretion, Holland is one of the safest countries in which to travel alone. You will find VVV offices everywhere and they are more than helpful. Should you require the police in an emergency, dial 22 22 22.

No-no's

Don't hitchhike on main roads — it's illegal. Outside of Amsterdam, it's also very competitive. Bear in mind, the Dutch rather frown on hitching and men will often take it as an invitation for more than a ride.

Don't walk around Zeedijk towards the harbour — it's an area for drug users. The rest of Amsterdam's notorious Red Light District is okay around Outezijds Voorburgwal, but there are sleazy sailors' bars, sex shops and prostitutes, so you may not feel comfortable without an escort.

Essentials

There is no essential you can't find in a Dutch shop which is often open as early as 8.30 a.m., and in resort areas will be open evenings and weekends. The best towns for shopping are Amsterdam, The Hague, Rotterdam and Eindhoven. Electricity is 220v, 50 cycles.

Medical Survival

Should you need medical assistance, call The Central Medical Service in Amsterdam, tel: 64 21 11 which will provide information on doctors, dentists and your nearest pharmacy location. Pharmacies rotate their opening hours — for information about weekend duty, tel: 13 28 55.

The standard of medical care is very high in Holland and most doctors do speak English. Since the country belongs to the EEC, it does have a reciprocal agreement with the UK to provide free medicine to British visitors holding an E111 form (see Introduction). Doctors are listed in the Dutch Yellow Pages under 'D' or 'M' (*medecins*).

What to do Solo

Holland is so full of easily reached delights that organised excursions are actually unnecessary. *Amsterdam* itself is a marvellous city for exploring on foot without getting lost whilst several canal boat companies offer trips lasting an hour or more — many starting from Dam Square.

The Dutch capital claims 40 museums so there's no lack of things to look at. One of the major ones is the Rijksmuseum, an art museum whose prime emphasis is on seventeenth-century Dutch Masters and which requires a minimum two hours' worth of browsing. The Van Gogh Museum is another must, housing one of the world's most complete collection of Van Gogh's paintings.

There are at least two breweries and several diamond cutters which offer free tours — samples are only available at the former! Of the city's outdoor markets, don't miss the Singel Flower Market or the famous flea market at Walkenburgerstraat.

Thanks to excellent transport and the country's minuscule size, day trips from the capital are effortless. Only a few miles away is *Aalsmeer* where you can watch flowers being auctioned any weekday morning right through the year. In under an hour, you can reach *Alkmaar*, one of Holland's three remaining 'cheese towns' still holding a traditional open-air cheese market every Friday morning between April and September. A special 'cheese train' will take you there. *Gouda* also holds a cheese market every Thursday morning in summer, using painted farm wagons instead of porters to transport it. *Delft* is another postcard-pretty town reached in under an hour, famous of course for its pottery.

The Hague is a far more elegant city than the capital — and is the seat of Holland's parliament. That seat, the Binnenhof, is its chief attraction, along with principal museums like the Gemeente (containing the world's largest collection of Mondrians) and the Mauritshuis. On The Hague's doorstep are two tourist attractions most visitors refuse to miss: *Madurodam*, a model village featuring every famous building and monument in the country — and *Scheveningen*, a seaside resort that offers Blackpool-style fun and sophisticated gambling.

Rotterdam doesn't have Amsterdam's photogenic appeal, but could be the destination for a business traveller. Almost entirely rebuilt after the Second World War, it is cosmopolitan — as a main European trading centre should be. It boasts a number of smart shops and restaurants, especially around pedestrian-zoned Lijnbaan. The Euromast Tower is the city landmark, giving the best overall city view. Pleasure cruisers leave for a harbour tour from Willemsplein landing stage. The most important museum is the Boymans-van Beuningen; the prettiest district, Delftshaven.

Marken and *Volendam* are often combined in one trip. Both villages are noted for their smoked eel houses and the colourful regional costume that their inhabitants sometimes wear. Although Holland is known as the land of windmills, the only real place to see any operating these days is at *Kinderdijk* on a Saturday afternoon in July/August. The time of year can naturally be important to sightseers: *Keukenhof*'s flower gardens in Lisse at the heart of the bulb belt are at their best April/May.

As tiny as it is, The Netherlands is divided into 12 provinces: they are Ijsselmeer, Gelderland, Noord Brabant, Friesland, Overijssel, Zuid-Holland, Noord-Holland, Drenthe, Groningen, Limburg, Zeeland and Utrecht.

Visas and Inoculations

Visa — none required.
Inoculations — none required.

Useful Addresses

Consulates
British Consulate, Koningslaan 44, 1007 AL Amsterdam. Tel: 76 43 43
US Consulate, Museumplein 19, 1071 DJ Amsterdam. Tel: 79 03 21

Tourist Offices
Netherlands Board of Tourism, 25/28 Buckingham Gate, London SW1. Tel: 01 828 7941
Netherlands Tourist Office, 575 Fifth Avenue, New York, NY 10036. Tel: (212) 245 5320

5 HUNGARY

Hungary, has never been totally independent: it was colonised by the Magyars in the ninth century and fell to the Turkish Empire in the sixteenth century. Nor is it independent today having been taken over by Russia in 1945, who turned it into a People's Republic. Hungary tried again for independence in 1956 but failed. That 'revolution' is bitterly remembered, even if the people don't like talking about it.

Unbroken in spirit, however, Hungary lives fairly happily and certainly happily welcomes tourists. Wine flows in the restaurants, food is delicious and the violins still play though most of the true gypsies have disappeared. Yugoslavia apart, the country is far less drab than other Socialist Bloc countries and, if Budapest's shops are anything to go by, can afford a better standard of life.

The Male Attitude

At first contact, there is little in common between today's Hungarians and the Magyars, much feared fighters of the past. But there is a bond: a lust for life, a fierce pride and loyalty to friends. Hungarians are passionate, generous and enthusiastic about most things. They go out on a limb to be helpful and possess that sense of fun and humour that even the heaviest socialist rules cannot suppress.

The single woman will find that assistance knows no bounds. She will be pestered only by flattery and possibly wooed. It is almost impossible not to fall in love with a Hungarian.

Where to Stay

There are excellent hotels in Budapest and Lake Balaton, the two main visitor destinations. Budapest particularly can offer luxury with a superb Hilton integrated into a castle, a Hyatt and an Intercontinental. Despite a flourish of new hotels in recent years, there is still a shortage of accommodation so advance booking is a necessity. Inexpensive hotels are unlikely to have bathrooms en suite.

HUNGARY

Getting Around on Your Own

It is safe and reliable! Car hire is available and there are some motorways: from Budapest to Győr on the way to Vienna; to Eastern Hungary; and to Balaton. Costs aren't cheap but bookings may be made through the state owned travel agency IBUSZ which has several branches.

Train travel is so cheap it always means crowds. Queues for tickets at railway stations are long so buy well in advance and reserve a seat. Scenically speaking, the three routes you are likely to take are: the line southeast to Yugoslavia, the line to and from Austria, or the line to Lake Balaton.

Buses are 'iffy'. The system is extensive enough but the frequency could be better, and fares are so low that vehicles are always jam-packed. Hitching is safely permitted but remember that Hungarians' cars are small.

Getting around the capital itself is easy once you've got the hang of it. Trams and buses will take you almost everywhere you care to go for painless prices. Tickets must be purchased beforehand, though, from tobacconists or special kiosks. The new metro is efficient and taxis are cheap but expect a tip. If you have difficulty finding a taxi to flag down, try the nearest hotel.

Eating and Drinking Solo

Who could feel ill at ease in Hungary's taverns, restaurants and cafés when they're all so lively? There are cafés called *eszpreszó* in practically every busy street, countless snack bars known as *ételbar* or *bisztró* plus self-service restaurants — *önkiszolgáló étterem*. But it would be a shame not to visit some of the old nostalgic places like Ruszwurm on Castle Hill in Budapest, the city's oldest pastry shop and bakery since the sixteenth century. Or Vörösmarty on Vörösmarty Square, the Pest side of the Danube where the choice of ice cream concoctions and marzipan confections is endless.

Restaurants spill onto pavements and terraces in summer when music is invariably played. Don't be dubious about entering a wine tavern either. They may look dark and offputting but there's always a jolly crowd inside.

Country inns called *czardas* serve good food in rustic settings. Expect plenty of paprika and sour cream in the food, all types of goulash, strudels and pancakes. Hungarian wines are some of Eastern Europe's best. Best known are Tokaj and Bull's Blood.

The Safety Factor

Providing you don't break the local rules, you'll find courtesy, help if you need it — and safety. The police number in Budapest is 07 but for any real problem it may be better to call your Embassy.

# No-no's

Don't camp anywhere but an authorised site — it's illegal.
Don't think tipping isn't necessary.

# Essentials

It isn't a problem to find make-up and toiletries but the only places to buy imported brands are in the 'tourist shops' where purchases must be made in 'hard currency' (i.e. foreign currency such as dollars or sterling). Most of the clothing is not up to the quality you are used to.

Electricity is 220v, 50 cycles.

# Medical Survival

A hotel will find an English-speaking doctor if necessary and no hospital will refuse initial aid, but medical insurance is advisable. Ambulance number in Budapest is 04.

# What to do Solo

Budapest is a city split by the Danube. Buda is the prettier, hillier castle district, easy to walk around in the vicinity of the Hilton where there are tiny shops and cafés and a view across the river from Fisherman's Bastion. Organ concerts are sometimes given in Matyas Cathedral and also at the Hilton itself.

Pest is the sprawling commercial part of the city with parks, monuments, shops and cafés. The most central square is Vörösmarty with pedestrian shopping precincts, like Váci Utca, radiating off it. The other popular boulevards are Lenin Körút, Múzeum Körút and the avenues of Rákóczi Utca and Népköztársaság Utca. See what the locals buy at one of the department stores such as Skála in Marx Square.

The best museum is the National, but there are others in City Park along with a lake and amusement areas. It is okay to walk through the park, though the lake water is not very clean. A more pleasant place to walk is Margaret Island in the Danube, reached by ferry. In summer, outside entertainment is given here.

Lake Balaton may be reached in a day's excursion with or without a guide. It is the Hungarians' 'seaside'. Resorts are located on both shores of the 42-mile-long lake whose waters are warm and clean (Siófok is the most popular centre). An indoor recommendation is winetasting in the cellars of Badacsony on Balaton's north shore.

Visas and Inoculations

Visa — required.
Inoculations — none required.

Useful Addresses

Embassies
British Embassy, Harmincad Utca 6, Budapest. Tel: 171 430
US Embassy, V. Szabadsag Ter 12, Budapest. Tel: 126 450
Hungarian Embassy, 35 Eaton Place, London SW1. Tel: 01 235 4048.

6 ITALY

In some ways Italy is not the ideal country in which to travel alone — the government is almost always in a state of turmoil; the economy frequently ails; public transport usually runs on whim; and waves of crime like bag snatching and kidnapping hit the press headlines.

Yet in some ways it is perfect — the cities, resorts, the food, the people, make it all worthwhile. With some caution and a lot of tolerance, any woman would find a visit here rewarding. It is well to bear in mind, though, that poverty is no fiction in Italy and even fast-paced cities like Milan and Turin have their slums. A reason no doubt why much of the country, especially the province of Emilia-Romagna, has inclinations towards communism.

For the tourist, it is probably the south which evidences the greatest contrast, sticking quite rigidly to old ways and customs. The area is less developed and open minded than the rest of the country and family feuds remain prevalent in places like Sicily and Sardinia.

Each Italian region is special. Piemonte, at the foot of the Alpes Maritimes, is rich in lakes, French influence and fine cuisine — and is an important commercial centre for the country. Lombardia is one of the most industrial regions of Italy but also claims summer and winter resorts. The same is true of Trentino and Alto Adige between Veneto and the Austrian border, sharing the Dolomites and Alpine lakes. Veneto is particularly varied and encompasses that most beloved destination — Venice. A wealth of famous seaside resorts are to be found in Liguria, an arc stretching from the French Riviera to Toscana. The highest mountains are in the regions of Abruzzi and Molise whilst Campania is the area surrounding Naples and Salerno. Lesser known Puglia forms Italy's 'heel' and Calabria is still perhaps the least touristically spoiled.

The Male Attitude

Ask anyone and they'll tell you that Italy is a woman's country in as much as Italian men love women! They do for sure, and at times this may prove bothersome. They are perseverant (albeit not in a nasty way) and if you don't want to know, you'll have to let them know in no uncertain manner. Funnily enough, however, the bottom-pinching days are long gone and this is not likely to be one humiliation (or thrill) you're liable to suffer. This change may be accounted for by the somewhat relaxed views on divorce and other moralities even though Italy retains its high degree of Catholicism.

The family is very important to Italians. Family honour has at times led to violence (e.g. the Mafia) but on the plus side, children are revered as much as the authentic Italian mama (on a par with the traditional Jewish mama). Watch an Italian family out for Sunday lunch and you'll see what I mean. And Sunday lunch is an *occasion*, for the Italians themselves adore food and wine, eating and drinking with great gusto.

True to Latin form, the Italians are volatile, bursting into floods of abuse (or affection) at the drop of a hat. Ordinary conversation has a noisy aggressive ring to it and two drivers verbally battling it out are straight out of a movie script. Laziness is another characteristic or often a shrug is *the* only answer (an expressive one, of course). This can work for or against you. Ask when the next train is due and that shrug may well be frustrating. Yet board a bus without the right change for the machine and a shrug may mean a free ride!

Where to Stay

Many of Italy's de luxe hotels are of the grande dame variety, maybe former *palazzas* like the Gritti in Venice, the kind of marbled establishment they can't afford to build any more with the kind of silver service it's hard to find. Because they offer you a protective ambience, top bracket hotels like CIGA's are recommended to the lone female. And by the way, they are not so snobby or stuffy as they once were.

At the lower end of the scale, look for the signs *albergo*, *pensione* or *soggiorno* but don't expect a standardised quality. Some are excellent — family-run, including breakfast in the room rate, providing a single room and a warm atmosphere. Some are terrible. A *pensione* in a tourist resort will not, of course, have the amenities of a large hotel, but can be a rewarding bargain — and this includes expensive Venice.

Getting Around on Your Own

Only the most confident should attempt to drive in Italy despite the fast *autostradas* which are well serviced. Local driving habits are atrocious, particularly in Rome, and you'll need all your courage and expertise.

Getting from one major city to another by train proves no problem — connections are frequent, fast and not that expensive, but otherwise, expect hassles. Neither the *locale* (which stops everywhere), nor the *diretto* (which stops almost everywhere) are exactly ideal if time is important to you — though I suspect no shortage of people willing to share their flagon of wine and salami sandwich with you. The *expresso* is quite a good fast train, stopping only at main stations but best is the *rapido*, operating between major towns. You will need a reservation for the latter and must pay a supplement, and in some cases it is first class only.

International and long distance trains all have restaurant cars and on most trains someone will come round selling snacks and soft drinks. Mobile food carts can also be found at big stations. On some lines like Milano-Venezia, Roma-Ventimiglia, Roma-Reggio Calabria, Roma-Bari and Milano-Roman, self-service restaurant cars have been introduced. Second class travel, by the way, is reasonable if not terribly comfortable.

If you're planning to travel extensively on Italian railways, ask about the Travel-at-will ticket which provides unlimited travel on the network for specified periods of time at a reduced rate. Be wary of the 'Circular' or 'Chilmetrico' tickets — these may not save you money.

Long-distance bus service is useful; inter-city buses are quite cheap; and city buses have a fixed fare. Ticket machines are on board or you can buy tickets at most tobacconists. Rome and Milan also have an underground system. From your point of view, getting around by bus can be difficult if you don't speak Italian, but it will be interesting.

Boat service to prime tourist destinations is a better bet. For instance, during the summer there are almost hourly steamer services from Naples to Capri, whilst car ferry services operate to Elba, Giglio, the Pontine, Aeolian, Lampedusa and Tremiti islands. There is a frequent boat service between points on Lake Maggiore and many lake cruises — both here and for Lake Como and on Lake Garda. As for Venice, you'll quickly get the hang of the *vaporetto, the* cheap, if crowded way to travel along the Grand Canal.

 Eating and Drinking Solo

Choose where to eat and drink alone by instinct. For example, you'll feel out of place in what is obviously a working men's bar, but the standup coffee bars (they also sell liquor) that proliferate all over Italy are fine. No one need feel ill at ease in any café including those around St Mark's Square in Venice or the Piazza Navona in Rome — or indeed at any nightspot though be prepared for the usual attentions.

Trattorias generally have a more casual atmosphere than a *ristorante* which could turn out to be anything from just another café to a break-the-budget de luxe eating place. At *rosticcerie* or a *tavola calda* you can order counter snacks. Look for the sign *menu touristico* if you seek a full meal at a fixed price.

Like France, Italian cuisine is very varied. Just remember there's more to pasta than spaghetti. Wines, too, since each region seems to produce its own type.

ITALY

 **The Safety Factor**

The biggest danger is bag or necklace snatching in the major cities, notably Rome and Palermo. Don't wear expensive jewellery, keep valuables in the hotel safe and wear your shoulder bag and camera seat-belt fashion. Beware of pickpockets especially on public transport. Male/female hassles are *de rigueur* but not dangerous. In fact, being a woman alone can have high benefits in Italy — a smile and a pretty face (feminists will have to forgive) will work wonders. Dial 113 for police emergencies.

 **No-no's**

Don't camp alone in deserted countryside (e.g. Sardinia).
Don't accept lifts.
Don't walk alone in non-touristy dark areas of any city.
Enquire locally about acceptable beach wear before stripping.
Don't wear shorts and do cover shoulders for church visits, especially in the south.
Don't even let yourself in on the fringe of the drug scene — the police come down like a ton of bricks.

 **Essentials**

In the large cities and resort areas, there's no shortage of essential goods or toiletries. Places like Rome, Milan, Florence and the top ski resorts all tend to be dressy, but since Italy is so fashionable, what you don't bring you can always buy. Basics and bargains are best bought at the chain stores: La Rinascente, Upim and Standa have branches in almost every town.

 **Medical Survival**

As a member of the EEC, the Italian health service has a reciprocal agreement with the British National Health Service. Visitors should take their E111 form to the nearest INAM (Instituto Nazionale per d'Assicorazione contro la Malattie) office and they'll issue the right certificate and list doctors on the scheme. Specialist and dental treatment is available from INAM surgeries, hospitals and some private clinics although part payment may be required for some drugs.

You'll find chemists (*farmacias*) in every town, all posting a list of those open at night and on weekends. A first aid service is available at airports, railway stations and hospitals. Emergency number in most destinations is 113.

What to do Solo

An organised sightseeing trip of *Rome* will at least orientate you, for there are many, many monuments and landmarks scattered throughout the city. It goes without saying that you'll see the Vatican and St Peter's, the Forum, Colosseum and Palatine Hill, and drop the necessary coins in the Fountain of Trevi. You may well want to stay a while in one of the three main squares which are just as busy at night as during the day: Piazza Navona, Piazza del Popolo and Piazza Santa Maria. You could sit for hours at a sidewalk café on the Via Veneto or by the Spanish Steps.

Don't, however, take an organised tour by night of Rome — it's boring. Rather go to a concert or listen to opera, outdoors in summer at the Terme di Caracella or at the opera house at Via Viminale in winter. To find out about specific events, buy 'This Week in Rome' or ask at the local tourist office.

For extravagant shopping (or window gazing) walk down Via Condotti, Via Borgognona, Via Frattina and Via della Vite. Your purse may be slightly less endangered if you wander along Via Tritone, Via del Corso, Via Ottaviano or Via Cola di Rienzo.

Milan's focal point is the *duomo* (cathedral) whose interior stained glass and rose windows are well worth looking at and whose roof is worth the climb. An evening at La Scala is a must. The actual opera season is usually over by May, having started in December, but there are evening concerts through to the middle of July. As for museums, Pinacoteca di Brera is one of the best.

Venice no doubt will make you wish you weren't on your own for, despite its summer heat and smells, its overpriced cafés in St Mark's Square and its gaudy souvenir stands, everyone falls in love with the place. But make the best of it: listen to the café orchestras, ask about tickets to the musical events at La Fenice Theatre, and take time to study the masterpieces at the Accademia which houses the cream of Venetian painting. Enjoy the illuminated view of the Church of Della Salute from the terrace of the Gritti Palace and indulge in a *bellini* (champagne with peach juice) at Harry's Bar. Walk the labyrinth of narrow streets in search of good leather and glass — there are exquisite items along with the mediocre if you're a discriminating purchaser.

Single women are often drawn to *Florence* — to paint, study, imbibe the arts. 'Italian Renaissance' was born and grew up here. The city boasts at least 40 museums and around a dozen great churches. You might start at the *duomo* — a splendid fifteenth-century cathedral — and end up at the magnificent Uffizi gallery whose art collection is one of the world's most superb. The Ponte Vecchio is lined with jewellery shops, and across it the Pitti Palace now houses several museums though it was once a Medici stronghold. San Lorenzo is one example of the Florentine churches and for ice cream with a view go to Piazzale Michelangelo.

For a restful holiday the *Lombardy lakes*: Como, Garda, Maggiore and Lugano are all fringed by resort hotels. Some people say the best cruise possibility is from *Stresa* to *Arona* and *Baveno*. For a sporty holiday *Cortina d'Ampezzo* is one of the poshest ski resorts with everything from gentle beginner slopes to Olympic jumps. Among the popular coastal resorts, *Rapallo* and *Lido de Jessolo* are well known, especially to the British market.

Visas and Inoculations

Visa — none required.
Inoculations — none required.

Useful Addresses

Embassies
British Embassy, Via XX Settembre 80a, Rome. Tel: 475 5441
US Embassy, Via Veneto 119a, 00187 Rome. Tel: 46742

Tourist Offices
Italian Tourist Office, 1 Princes Street, London W1. Tel: 01 408 1254
Italian Tourist Office, 630 Fifth Avenue, New York, NY 10011. Tel: (212) 245 4961

7 MALTA

This strange, small, dry little historic island is a favourite holiday destination with the British, thanks to a year-round temperate climate and the fact that it's a rare Maltese who doesn't speak English. The Knights of St John built its palaces and churches, defending their fortress against Turkish invaders. The British came at the beginning of the nineteenth century and stayed until 1964 when the island won its independence. Afterwards, the British were tempted back (this time on holiday) by low prices. Despite political moves at certain times in recent years to make the English feel unwelcome, the island has not ceased to realise its economy was based on tourism, most of which stemmed from the UK.

Principally a catholic country, Malta remains a welcoming country, a compact and friendly haven for the single female tourist.

The Male Attitude

Like many another Catholic-influenced destination, the Maltese attitude can be hypocritical. Abroad, they do have an unfortunate reputation for dabbling in drugs and prostitution yet on their own island, they are protective of family and hospitable to strangers.

At heart, the Maltese man has a Latin nature — headstrong and passionate, quarrelsome and emotional. Taken at face value, he is polite, sometimes cautious. Should you accept a date from a local, be aware that upfront chivalry can slip fast given half a chance. Also be aware that in recent years, the Arabs (Libyans in particular) have discovered the merits of this island on their doorstep. They do stay in the best hotels, frequent the plusher bars and *their* attitude to a woman sitting alone on a bar stool may not be the one you'd wish for. So be careful what you say 'yes' or 'no' to.

Where to Stay

There is really no such thing as a pension in Malta, but there are tourist class hotels as well as top class ones such as the Hilton, Dragonara and Corinthia Palace. In recent years, self-catering has also become a major attraction now that apartment and villa complexes have mushroomed throughout the island. Nowhere can be considered isolated and there is no lack of shops selling familiar foods.

Getting Around on Your Own

Car hire is easy and compared to other destinations, cheap, but rental cars do tend to be the battered variety. Distances are short so it's almost impossible to get lost and everyone is willing to tell you the way. Only parking poses a problem if one discounts the erratic driving of the Maltese themselves. They rarely keep to official speed limits (25 mph in towns, 40 mph outside), often preferring to drive in the middle of the road rather than on the official left.

Failing motoring, buses are the best way to get from place to place. They're cheap, easy to locate and use, linking as they do all the towns and villages with Valletta's terminal outside Freedom Gate.

Water taxis ply the Grand Harbour in Valletta and a passenger/car ferry links Malta with her sister islands, Gozo and Comino.

Eating and Drinking Solo

It's unlikely you'll ever feel you're in the wrong place at the wrong time in Malta since so many other tourists choose it. Cafés, tea shops, restaurants, pubs and discos can be found in every resort centre, all quite charming, none seedy. International fare, from hamburgers to fish and chips, is as available as Maltese specialities like *timpani*, a sort of lasagne. Maltese wines are pleasant enough and, by the glass, less expensive than a coffee.

The Safety Factor

No problems, even at night in any of the tourist centres, e.g. Sliema, St Paul's Bay, Mellieha or St Julian's, where tourist facilities are clustered and well patronised.

No-no's

Don't wear clothes which are too revealing, nor anything too abbreviated, for visiting churches. Shorts are not allowed.
Expect to be asked to dance or be offered a drink in the better hotel cocktail bars — deal firmly with unwanted attention.
Don't expect sandy beaches except in the north.

Essentials

British goods are readily available. The widest range is for sale in

Valletta's shops but remember stores generally close for lunch and an afternoon siesta period, reopening in the late afternoon. Valletta's main shopping street, Kingsway, is pedestrianised at certain times of the day.

Leave the tiara at home. Nowhere on this island (including the casino) is that dressy.

Electricity is 240v, 50 cycles.

Medical Survival

Imported pharmaceuticals are easy to find at reasonable prices. Doctors usually speak English — your hotel will call one if necessary. Hygienic standards are high and the tap water is safe to drink.

What to do Solo

Doing anything on your own in Malta is reasonable enough. You don't need to be in a group to browse through *Valletta* whose cathedral contains Caravaggio's masterpiece, 'The Beheading of St John'. The earliest Grand Masters of the Order of St John are buried in the crypt here and a collection of the Knights' weapons is on display in the Armory at the Palace of the Grand Masters.

The island's old capital, *Mdina* has to be seen on foot as well. Within the walled city is a duplicate cathedral and, practically hidden, tiny shops and café restaurants wedged into narrow cobbled streets. Mdina's suburb of *Rabat* boasts the Malta Crafts Centre, a collection of buildings where silverwork, glass, pottery and other items are made and sold. (For bargains, look at the 'seconds' shelf in the Mdina Glass Factory.)

A hired car (or bus) will take you to a photographers' delight — *Marsaxlokk*, a fishing village whose *luzzu* boats are brightly coloured, or Malta's archaeological sites like the underground temples of *Tarxien*. Or Mostar Church whose huge dome was penetrated by an unexploded bomb in the Second World War, miraculously saving a packed congregation from death.

Getting to *Gozo* is simple — ferries leave from Sliema's waterfront but to explore this more peaceful green and hilly island, wheeled transport is required.

Visas and Inoculations

Visa — none required.
Inoculations — none required.

Useful Addresses

High Commission
British High Commission, 7 St Anne Street, Floriana. Tel: 621 285

Tourist Offices
Malta Government Tourist Office, 1 City Arcade, Valletta. Tel: 24444
Malta Government Tourist Office, College House, Wrights Lane, London W8. Tel: 01 938 2668

8 PORTUGAL

Portugal has changed little over the years. It is still basically a Catholic country where community feeling matters and the family is a stronghold. Developers may have moved in on the Algarve creating homes for foreigners, but the Portuguese themselves have a strong sense of history and tradition.

In rural aras, old women with creased faces, continue to wear black, frown on abbreviated dress and lack of morals, and work as hard as they have always done. For all their hard work, though, the pace outside of Lisbon is an unhurried one which may be enjoyed by the truly independent traveller.

The country was wrested from the Moors in the twelfth and thirteenth centuries but only after many years, so it is not surprising that a Moorish influence lingers on and is particularly evident in some of the architecture.

The Male Attitude

No longer the wealthy country it was at the time of the conquests in the New World, Portugal has suffered from high unemployment and inflation which resulted in a communistic streak, so expect to find 'leftish' viewpoints and outlook. That is not to say that the people aren't friendly — they are — and hold strong ties with the British in particular.

The Portuguese man is a typical continental male who expects his women to do things for him, his way. He will woo and cajole charmingly to win a bride, but once married is less inclined to flattery. His mother and his children more than likely take priority over his wife.

If a Portuguese male is a pest to the visting woman from abroad, it is merely determination to show superiority and win, but firm handling will be respected and the man who remains an escort can be amusing and thoughtful company.

Where to Stay

Portugal has its shares of luxury hotels in major cities and along the celebrated Algarve coast, but the woman who prefers more intimate surroundings is better off in one of the countless pensions or *pousadas*. The latter are state owned, well maintained and efficiently run, usually located in areas of touristic interest and are sometimes conversions of historic buildings. Private inns are known as *estalagems* which are also scattered around the country and are an excellent choice. More recently, manor houses began to offer bed and breakfast accommodation in rural areas, but rates are not necessarily lower.

The self-caterer will find the Algarve her best bet. Over the last decade or so, clusters of villas and holiday apartments have sprung up around tiny coastal fishing villages, and golf courses. These complexes, complete with supermarkets and sport facilities, include some of the best designed in Europe where no one would feel stranded.

Getting Around on Your Own

By car is the best answer even though not all roads are that good and Portuguese driving can be appallingly fast and furious, as it is in Lisbon. In those towns with old quarters (e.g. Lisbon or Oporto) roads are narrow and finding a parking spot can be frustrating. Petrol, too, is costly.

Although the country is well served with trains, the only decent services are the Lisbon-Algarve and Oporto-Coimbra-Lisbon lines, since others are rather slow and tend to run at inconvenient times. Express bus service operates between major cities and within cities there is a reasonably good local bus service. Local bus service along the Algarve is not dependable.

Eating and Drinking Solo

Don't be afraid to brave a restaurant because it looks 'tired' or basic. What may appear to be a hole-in-the wall often turns out to be the best choice. Lisbon's old coffee houses with their marble-topped tables and high ceilings are ideal places in which to spend time alone. There are cheap restaurant-cafés on the Rua da Palma and Rua da Madalena but avoid the working-class bars. Smart cafés are in the Rossio and the Chiado — don't be put off by the fact that much of the patronage is male.

Portuguese men are always the ones to appear to be doing very little and local women seldom appear in bars on their own, but that doesn't mean you won't be tolerated. The *Casas de fado* are often frequented by people on their own if only for the fact one comes to listen to plaintive melodies and definitely *not* to talk. Meals aren't obligatory in such establishments and you can sit for hours over a glass of house wine. The Portuguese do eat late and keep late hours, however, so fado houses don't fill up until 11 p.m. or so.

The food is rather bland and unimaginative. Fish is a staple whether it be *bacalhau* (practically a national dish of salted cod) or grilled sardines. *Caldo verde*, a cabbage and potato soup, frequently appears on menus and pork is the most often listed meat. In any of the minuscule country places in the north or in the hills above the Algarve, three course meals with wine are surprisingly cheap. Wine drinkers can have a field day with a wide choice of regional wines including the *vinho verdes* (young slightly sparkling) and the king of all, port.

The Safety Factor

If you take normal precautions, there are no procedures or places you have to avoid. You dial 36 61 41 for the police if necessary in Lisbon and in an emergency 115 anywhere in the country.

No-no's

Don't talk during a fado.
Don't wear shorts or other inappropriate dress to visit churches.
Don't confuse the word *bica* (black coffee) with *pica* (a 'joint').
Don't stay in *dormidas* — only down-and-outs do.

Essentials

Northern Portugal has an Atlantic climate, the south, Mediterranean, so choice of clothing will depend upon destination. Lisbon is a reasonably dressy city but Algarve living is casual. Any requisites you need (including sun creams and toiletries) can be bought readily in both places.

Electricity is 210-220v in most cases but 110v in some parts of the country.

Medical Survival

A number of doctors speak English and medicines are available, if expensive. Local drinking water is safe.

What to do Solo

Compared with other capital cities, *Lisbon* is compact. Its central quarter is not difficult to walk around — good shopping streets lead from the heart of it, the Rossio. Most interesting is the Alfama quarter, a twisting maze of cobbled streets and archways, terraces and courtyards. You'll have less chance of getting lost if you first pick up a suggested stroll itinerary from the tourist office. From the square of

Miradouro you can see the Alfama, the harbour below, and further along the Castelo São Jorge. Lisbon's main boulevard is Avenida da Liberdade which eventually leads to the formal Parque Eduardo V11.

Lisbon's two most important art museums are the Museu Nacional de Arte Antigua and the Gulbenkian. Lovers of markets will find the largest and best for food not far from Caes de Sodre station, the Thieves Market in the Campo de Sta, and flower stalls in the Rossio.

It takes a 20 minute train ride to reach the doorstep resorts of *Cascais* and *Estoril*. The former is best for bathing beaches but there is also a fisherman's beach where the catch is duly landed and hauled off to the fish market.

Northern Portugal is touring country, perhaps starting from *Oporto*, the country's second city, a major port divided by the Douro River. Best thing to do here is to visit one of the famous port cellars. By car it's easy to reach *Ofir*, an up and coming beach resort, plus the rest of the Costa Verde.

Southern Portugal is the beach choice. Anywhere along the *Algarve* is suitable, since there are sport facilities at any of the resorts. The most popular is *Albufeira*; the largest town is *Faro*. No centre is too big to walk around but transport is necessary to travel from resort to resort.

Visas and Inoculations

Visa — none required.
Inoculations — none required.

Useful Addresses

Embassies
British Embassy, Rua S. Domingos à Lupa 37, Lisbon. Tel: 66 11 91
US Embassy, Avenida das Forcas Armadas, Lisbon. Tel: 726 6600

Tourist Offices
Portuguese National Tourist Office, 1/5 New Bond Street, London W1. Tel: 01 493 3873
Portuguese Tourist Office, 548 Fifth Avenue, New York, NY 10036. Tel: (212) 354 4403

9 ROMANIA

I'd be lying if I said Romania was anything but fascinating, from its Black Sea coast to its Moldavian painted monasteries, but it suffers from the same bureaucracy as its socialist neighbours and shows the same inadequacies. The do's and don'ts are sometimes difficult to sort out as Romania has tried very hard to encourage tourism, partially succeeding at least for its coastal areas which are inclined to a British market.

Though the Western visitor invariably receives preferential treatment despite say food shortages elsewhere, one can't but help feel the frustrations of slow service and long queues and subjection to paperwork. In practical terms, a solo woman is better off visiting this country on a package holiday.

The Male Attitude

It is not really surprising that in a country with such a troubled history the Romanians should be cautious. Whatever his motivations, the Romanian's hospitality will if anything over extend his budget although promises to make sure something vital is done are more often made to soothe than to be kept. The educated men you meet will be attentive, courteous and considerate but you can expect to be ignored by many.

Where to Stay

Hotel standards are no way as high as in the West. Service is slow and plumbing often goes wrong even in the best hotels. The Intercontinental is probably the best in Bucharest. Most of the Black Sea resort hotels have been built for tourist groups and have adequate facilities, if lacking in style. Romania is most famous for its spas: important ones may be found at Eforie Nord, Mangalia and Neptun on the coast and Felix, Herculane, Calimanesti and Vatra Dornei inland.

Getting Around on Your Own

Romania's train system is improving and there are some express trains (for which reservations are compulsory). The main routes stem from the capital, Bucharest, but there is a trunk line also to the Black Sea resorts. Biggest problems for train travel are language and long, long queues for tickets. The country has an extensive local bus service — often the only way to see rural areas. Bucharest is served by bus, trolley bus and tram; tickets are sold at street corner kiosks.

Roads are also improving and maps are free from tourist offices, but shortages may require purchasing petrol on a tourist coupon system with 'hard' currency.

Getting around an actual coastal resort on your own is not difficult. Mamaia especially has a nine mile shoreline bordered by hotels, shops and sport facilities. Group tour excursions are made by coach.

Eating and Drinking Solo

In the tourist areas outdoor cafés and wine gardens are plentiful though service is slow and not all items on menus may be available at any given time. Romania is very group-conscious so that arranged evenings out at a local restaurant or folkloric club may actually be the simplest way to enjoy the cuisine.

Charcoal-grilled meats and sausages are a firm favourite; eggs and sour cream are frequently added to soups; cheese pies and sweet cream cheesecakes often appear. Some of Romania's best wines come from vineyards near the Black Sea.

The Safety Factor

As in most socialist countries, a fair degree of safety is assured and so long as you don't break local laws, treatment is courteous. The police phone number in Bucharest is 055 or in an emergency 061. A real problem necessitates a call to your Embassy.

No-no's

Don't believe the 'no tipping' policy; small gifts of makeup or tights are still well accepted by guides or chambermaids.
Don't change money on the black market — it could result in a trip to the police but even more likely you'll be ripped off by the locals.
Don't hitch alone.

 ## Essentials

You won't find Western brands of make up and toiletries in the shops whose goods are still rather poor quality. Take all you need with you. The only stores selling imported perfumes, liquor and cigarettes are the 'tourist shops' which accept only 'hard' currency.

Climatic conditions vary regionally: the Black Sea coast is obviously at its best in summer, Bucharest in spring. It is always cooler in the Carpathians (Romania's wintersport area).

Electricity is 220v, 50 cycles in most places.

 ## Medical Survival

Your own first aid kit and sufficient medical insurance are advisable. If necessary, a hotel will help find an English-speaking doctor and Bucharest has an all night pharmacy on Boulevard Magheru.

 ## What to do Solo

Busiest part of *Bucharest* is the area around Calea Victoriei, the location of goverment buildings, museums and shopping centres. Just off Calea Victoriei is the old Lipiscani district whose narrow streets wind around the Old Princely Court. The city is a gracious one with many fine boulevards, gardens and courtyards. Herastrau Park is the local recreational area for swimming, boating and lakeside restaurants. On the edge of the park, the Village Museum shows genuine peasant houses from all parts of the country.

Sunning and bathing are the key elements of the *Black Sea* resorts. The string of resorts starts at Constanza and includes Eforie Nord which has all categories of hotels, minigolf, tennis and motor boat trips on Lake Techirghiol, Mamaia (the most popular) and Neptun.

Transylvania is most famous for Bran Castle always associated with Count Dracula legends. Braşov on the edge of the Carpathians is the usual tourist base and gateway to the ski areas.

Moldavia is a particularly intriguing region noted for its painted monasteries. Interiors and exteriors are literally covered with frescoes — Voronet and Sucevita Monasteries are among the most beautiful and famous. Moldavia is equally a region for crafts, especially its unusual black pottery. A popular tourist base is Suceava.

 ## Visas and Inoculations

Visa — required.
Inoculations — none required.

Useful Addresses

Embassies
British Embassy, Strada Jules Michelet 24, 70154 Bucharest. Tel: 11 16 34
US Embassy, Strada Tudor Arghezi 7-9, Bucharest. Tel: 10 40 40
Romanian Embassy, 1 Belgrave Square, London SW1. Tel: 01 235 0388

10 SCANDINAVIA

No matter how the individual countries try, Denmark, Norway and Sweden are frequently lumped together to form Scandinavia. There are similarities: in their language, their food, their personality. Unspoiled countryside (often rugged terrain), a freedom of manner and expression, a certain coolness (though not aloofness) are common to all three. A high cost of living (and to visitors) is common to all three.

Scandinavians are not always blond as we would believe them to be, but they are almost all hardy types ready to brave the most hazardous outdoors at the drop of a bikini; adventurously sporty and disgustingly healthy. There is a sense of timing and precision about all the Nordic countries, a hygienic 'well scrubbed' atmosphere. It is evidenced in their design — modern clean cut lines and simplicity for everything from furniture to jewellery.

True or not, one feels the Nordic countries are well balanced, well adjusted and not very frivolous. Little Denmark, gateway to Scandinavia is wealthy but not pretentious, putting great emphasis on efficiency and social services. Scenically grand Norway is as open and clear as its glacial lakes. Neutral Sweden manages to combine affluence with social conscience, concentrating on the one hand on consumer goods, boasting on the other an effective welfare service.

The Male Attitude

Don't mistake a Scandinavian's cool, clipped, courteous approach for coldness. Nor should you discount him as unworrisome. Scandinavians are stubborn and can go to extremes. Who else would jump out of a sauna and into an icy pool in winter and consider it invigorating? Scandinavians have promoted the idea of health clubs, were the first to push for nudist beaches abroad, were the first to escape formality. (Even Royalty is casual in this part of the world.)

They share a hard working attitude and love of efficiency. Yet their warmth and generosity is as outstanding as their ability to party. The cheerful Danes feel close to the British, do what they promise, believe in sexual freedom and are similarly open minded about other subjects. Norwegians, both courageous and perseverant, are a nation of individualists bound together for their common good. Their mixture of common sense and good humoured sense of fun may confuse you at first but you'll soon find that what you thought was dull is anything but. (What Viking could be dull!) The reserved and conservative Swedes are actually a curious people, interested in their overseas visitors and far less clinical in outlook than some people would suppose.

Where to Stay

De luxe hotels are not a key Scandinavian feature. In their eyes, silver service does not go hand in hand with social welfare. They are much more inclined to modest but scrupulously clean lodgings or the simple comforts of a rustic lakeside cabin. That is not to say that the business guest won't find an aristocratic place to stay (e.g. Copenhagen's D'Angleterre, Oslo's Grand or Stockholm's Sheraton).

More spartan lodgings don't have to be uncomfortable. Country inns are genuinely welcoming; country cottages are readily available for summer rents; and the modestly priced 'Mission Hotels' (nothing to do with religion) are a boon for those on a budget without being in the least run down and seedy.

The land, like the people, is rugged so camping is well catered for.

Getting Around on Your Own

Fine for women. Emphasis on cleanliness, people who speak English, transport that operates as it should — all adds up to an enviable system. Standards are so high that second class rail travel can be regarded without worry and whilst speeds are not as fast as in some other destinations, service is tops. The separate countries have co-operatively created the 'Nordturist' runaround ticket which allows unlimited travel for 21 days on all the railways in Scandinavia plus travel on railway-operated bus routes outside of cities, and railway-operated ferries.

Rural Scandinavia depends on the bus service so nowhere becomes too out-of-the-way to reach.

Travel by car is probably the best way to see the most in a short time though the drink-and-drive laws are some of the most militant to be found anywhere. (If you should be involved in an accident, a blood test is given as a matter of course and the merest sign of alcohol could well result in a lengthy prison spell.) As for the roads, they're excellent in Denmark, recommended if they're major highways between cities in Sweden or Norway.

Naturally, boat travel is almost inescapable in countries boasting so many fjords and lakes. There are daily sailings between Copenhagen and Oslo and from Jutland in Denmark it's possible to cross directly into Norway and Sweden. Hydrofoils are utilised a great deal, especially in Norway, but for visitors it is the famous Scandinavian coastal cruises which are an essential attraction.

Eating and Drinking Solo

One can't help thinking of Scandinavia without thinking of a *smörgasbord* and frankly that can be enjoyed at any time of day. Scandinavian breakfasts, for instance, tend to be more varied than the normal European continental breakfast with the addition of cheeses and cold meats and herring. *Smörgasbord* is also the open sandwich or an evening buffet table.

In most large cities, sidewalk stands sell the Nordic equivalent of hot dogs — look for signs reading *Pølser* or *Varm Korv*. Restaurants display their prices outside so you won't be too shocked by the final bill. Many Scandinavians dine early having lunched early, around midday.

Their proximity to the sea no doubt has given the Scandinavians their love for fish and seafood dishes are as varied as they are excellent. Lobster, salmon and trout are all great favourites. Best places for coffee and pastries are the *Konditori*; best places for aquavit, literally everywhere! Aquavit, the local firewater, is generally drunk as an aperitif, downed with several 'skals'. If it's a little rough on the throat, an ice cold beer should soothe and Danish Carlsberg or Tuborg or Norwegian Ringnes or Schou are known throughout the world.

Liveliest Scandinavian city for nightlife is Copenhagen. The free publication 'This Week in Copenhagen' will show you current listings of what's on. Small music and dance spots can be found in the district around Nikolaj Kirke but skip the sailors' quarter of Nyhavn.

The Safety Factor

Use common sense and you won't find anywhere in Scandinavia threatening. Possibly the only big worry is getting lost in the mountains or feeling too lonely in one of the outlying sections of Scandinavia. Police emergency number in Denmark is 000; in Oslo it's 66 90 50, or 20 10 90 for an ambulance; and in Stockholm, 90000.

No-no's

Don't camp in an unauthorised place in Denmark.
Don't go unescorted to Copenhagen's Nyhavn district.
Don't expect to hitchhike easily anywhere in Norway.
Don't expect Gröna Lund (Stockholm's Tivoli) to be fantastic.
Don't expect to drink alcohol in 'Mission Hotels'.

Essentials

Shops in all major cities stock supplies of everything you might need, but be prepared for exorbitant prices.

Electricity is 220v, 50 cycles in most parts of Scandinavia.

Medical Survival

Most doctors speak English throughout Scandinavia and imported pharmaceuticals are readily available, if expensive. Drinking water is safe everywhere.

An emergency case will get free medical help from the casualty wards of most Danish hospitals and medical treatment for accidents or sudden illnesses are most often free as well. It will cost a few hundred kroner to call an emergency doctor on 0041. In Copenhagen, 24-hour pharmacies include Steno Apotek on Vesterbrogade, tel: 14 82 66 and Sonderbro Apotek on Amagerbrogade, tel: 58 01 40. There is usually a small surcharge for night service.

Norway has a reciprocal arrangement with the British National Health Service, but here again imported medicines are expensive. For emergency medical help go to Oslo's First Aid Centre on Storgaten, tel: 20 10 90 — it's open 24 hours. The Jerbanetorget Apotek is a 24-hour pharmacy.

Sweden's medical care is of an extremely high standard and prescription drugs are readily available. Emergency medical number is 90000. In Stockholm, the Apoteke C.K. Scheele on Klarabergsgatan, is open 24 hours, tel: 24 82 80.

What to do Solo

Walking round *Copenhagen* on foot is a pleasure in itself — during the summer months there are organised walking tours of Denmark's capital. As an alternative, hire a bike through the tourist office or from the railway station. As in Holland, cycling is a local passion.

One of the liveliest streets is Frederiksberggade; one of the largest department stores is Magasin du Nord at Kongens Nytorv; the local flea market takes place on Saturday mornings at Israels Plads behind Norreport Station. Guided tours will take you around the harbour or along the canals departing from Nyhavn Canal and from Gammel Strand and Christianshavn may be reached by water or on foot.

The Mechanical Music Museum is one of the city's more novel and if you like beer, you're in luck, both Carlsberg and Tuborg Breweries give free tours and samples. At the heart of the city, Tivoli Gardens is a world-famous safe-to-visit amusement park where free concerts are often held. Summer evenings sometimes finish with a brilliant firework display.

The most popular excursion out of Copenhagen takes visitors to Elsinore (Hamlet's Castle), a 15 minute train ride away, and on to Frederiksborg Castle, 35 minutes further on, housing fine old Danish furniture and paintings. Several seaside resorts surround Elsinore of which the most popular are Hillerød and Fredensborg.

The activity area of *Oslo* lays around pedestrianised Karl Johans Gate. If you stroll down the Wharf from the City Hall, you'll reach Akershus Castle, all of it open for inspection. Take the ferry from the City Hall across the harbour to the island of Bygday to see the Folk and Viking Museums. The best of the modern artist, Edvard Munch, can be seen in the Munch Museum as well as in the National Gallery. Best view of Oslo Fjord and city is from the top of the radio tower.

Norway's scenery is its biggest natural asset and touring fjord country is practically a must. By using a combination of ferries, buses and trains, you can make your way from Oslo to Stavanger, Bergen and the fjords beyond. Norway is so mountainous that skiing can be done practically everywhere, Oslo's own Nordmarka hills are a popular winter centre whilst Mongsberg and Klekken are two other ski resorts within easy reach of the capital.

Stockholm's modern centre lies between Sergels Törg and Hötorget but the old quarter of Gamla Stan is more colourful, and is also the location of the Royal Palace. The two finest art museums are on Skeppsheolmen: the National and the Museum of Modern Art. Another capital attraction is Skansen on the island of Djurgärden which features an open air display of old Swedish buildings and crafts.

Shopping stop might be at Nordiska Kompaniet on Hamngatan, a Harrods-style department store crammed with beautifully designed goods. A REA (or sale) could be tempting here. Stockholm's outdoor markets operate year round; one colourful one is in front of the Concert House, another on Östermalm.

In summer harbour and canal tours are possible and there are escorted walking tours of the Old Town. Don't miss the sauna experience — in your own hotel or at Sturebadet where you can choose a swim and steam bath or the full sauna treatment.

Visas and Inoculations

Visa — none required.
Inoculations — none required.

Useful Addresses

Embassies
British Embassy, Skarpogatan 628, Stockholm, Sweden: Tel: 67 01 40
British Embassy, Ths. Heftyesgate 8, Oslo 1, Norway. Tel: 52 24 00
British Embassy, Kastelsvej 36-40, Copenhagen DK 2100, Denmark. Tel: 26 46 00
US Embassy, Strandvagen 101, Stockholm, Sweden. Tel: 78 35 300
US Embassy, Drammensveien 18, Oslo 2, Norway. Tel: 44 85 50
US Embassy, Dag Hammarskjolds Alie 24, Copenhagen DK 2100, Denmark. Tel: 42 31 44.

Tourist Offices

Swedish National Tourist Office, 3 Cork Street, London W1. Tel: 01 437 5816

Norwegian Tourist Board, 20 Pall Mall, London SW1. Tel: 01 839 2650

Danish Tourist Board, 169/173 Regent Street, London W1. Tel: 01 734 2637

Swedish Tourist Office, 655 Third Avenue, New York, NY 10017. Tel: (212) 949 2333

Danish Tourist Office, 655 Third Avenue, New York, NY 10017. Tel: (212) 949 2333

Norwegian Tourist Office, 655 Third Avenue, New York, NY. 10017. Tel: 949 2333

11 THE SOCIALIST BLOC

To visit any soviet bloc country is an experience but one recommended only for the very thick-skinned woman if she is travelling by herself. The frustrations of long waits at airports, masses of paperwork, interminable queues, bad service and hassles in ordering or paying by credit card, are far too much for the average person.

Having said that there is not one country which would refuse tourism and even package tours allow you some freedom in which to explore. These days Western music has permeated everywhere and jeans are a common sight. Visitors won't be slapped in gaol for talking to local residents and aren't restricted to eating only in their own hotel.

The common factor is lack of quality and shortage of goods. One only has to compare the limited range in a Moscow or Sofia department store with that of a London or New York counterpart to realise how well off the West is. Packing decent soap, toilet paper, shampoo, etc. is practical. Taking coffee bags, biscuits and chocolate a recommendation.

Turning up, hiring a car and heading off is no simple matter, indeed almost impossible since pre payment of transport and accommodation is required before entry is permitted. A visa is necessary and there appears to be no rhyme or reason for a refusal to issue one.

Russia itself, however, was practically the first to open doors to tourists and since the early days of Thomson Holidays packages to Moscow, the country has been busy opening up more and more of its destinations for inspection. The charm is in the previously unknown, previously forbidden. To tour Moscow's Kremlin or Leningrad's L'Hermitage has proved fascinating enough for Westerners to flock *en masse*.

Bulgaria was more slow than Romania to heed the selling point of its own Black Sea coastline. Once they woke up to the fact they concentrated on developing beaches that stretch for 100 miles from Sozopol north to Balchic. Czechoslovakia has begun to woo the West, too, to its spas and Tatra mountains. Poland would be a little more enthusiastic if it had the money, though once inside this country regulations are the most relaxed of all.

THE SOCIALIST BLOC

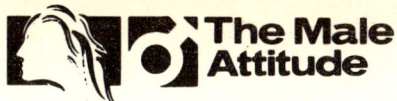
The Male Attitude

Bureaucracy at its worst is a certain bet. If coffee has not been ordered for a group's breakfast, no cajoling will obtain it. Restaurant and bar opening times listed in hotels are not adhered to. Explanations are not given when arrangements cannot be made. These are all attitudes to expect in Russia, Bulgaria, Czechoslovakia and, most of all, in East Germany.

On the other hand, the people are not unhelpful. A Russian waiter off duty may chat you up in order to practise his English. The Czech waiter is the first to change money on the black market — and the safest person to change it with. The easygoing Poles are the first to queue up at Pewex 'hard' currency shops for radios and washing machines.

If they all seem to be hard drinkers, perhaps one can understand why. Russians in particular drink to get drunk rather than to have a good time. The Poles traditionally are the most hospitable.

Where to Stay

Moscow hotels look like giant concrete boxes from the outside and from the inside, with cavernous dining rooms. 'Hard' currency bars are designated for tourists and coffee shops when they exist are invariably tucked away on an upper floor and don't serve tea. In Bulgaria, any establishment classified as an 'Interhotel' has been given special assistance so that it should conform to international standards. Some, like the Novotel Europe or Vitosha-New Otani in Sofia, are affiliated to well known chains. Likewise, there are 'Interhotels' in Czechoslovakia run by Cedok the state owned travel agency. In Poland look for Orbis hotels which include foreign-built luxury ones like Intercontinental and Holiday Inns.

Getting Around on Your Own

Unquestionably difficult, though possible with the aid of a holiday representative and/or tourist office (state run). Getting around the cities is usually by tram or bus (Moscow and Prague both have metro systems) or by organised sightseeing tour.

Eating and Drinking Solo

In many cases, eating out at a restaurant is available on a pre-paid voucher system with a booking made by the state travel organisation (e.g. Intourist in Russia). Don't expect everything listed on the menu to be available, but do expect lots of iced vodka and Georgian wines to be included in the meal price. Prague's wine taverns have a good atmosphere (more amenable to women than the equally prevalent beer taverns) and attract a young crowd. Warsaw's cafés (they move outdoors in summer) are suitably safe and reliable.

 **Essentials**

Take everything with you, especially items like tampax. Hairdressers exist but shampoos, conditioners, hairsprays, etc. may not be of very high standard.

 **Medical Survival**

Necessary medicines and first aid items are best brought with you. In the case of a medical emergency, your holiday company rep. is your number one friend. Drinking only bottled water is a wise (sometimes imperative) precaution.

 **What to do Solo**

Seeing the sights requires organised arrangements, either in a group or with a personal guide. Suggestions of what you might do on your own, however, are as follows: in *Moscow*, walk to Red Square (most tourist hotels are near it) and admire St Basil's fairytale appearance but don't go at midnight if only not to run into drunken Moscovites. Push your way through GUM, *the* department store, comprising numerous small stores all under one roof, but purchases here may only be made in roubles.

In summer in *Sofia*, outdoor concerts are given in Liberty Park. Listen to the choir in Alexander Nevsky Memorial Church or ask about tickets to a performance by the National Folk Ensemble. Best view in *Prague* is from Castle Square, from where you can walk to the Lesser Town and Old Town. One of the city's most appealing events is the Spring Music Festival.

Warsaw's only district with character is the Old Town, razed during the Second World War but painstakingly resurrected exactly as it was by studying Canaletto paintings of how it used to look. For craft shopping, look out for the Cepelia chain of stores.

 **Visas and Inoculations**

Visa — required for any of the socialist bloc countries.
Inoculations — none required.

Useful Addresses

Embassies

British Embassy, Naberezhnaya Marisa Toreza 14, Moscow 72, USSR. Tel: 231 85 11
British Embassy, Thunovska 14, 11800 Prague, Czechoslovakia. Tel: 53 33 47
British Embassy, Aleje Roz 1, 00556 Warsaw, Poland, Tel: 281 001
British Embassy, Unter den Linden 32-34, 108 Berlin, East Germany. Tel: 220 2431
British Embassy, Boulevard Marshall, Tolbukhin 65-67, Sofia, Bulgaria. Tel: 885 5361
US Embassy, Ulitsa Chaykovskogo 19-23, Moscow, USSR. Tel: 252 24 51
US Embassy, Trziste 15, 12548 Prague, Czechoslovakia. Tel: 53 66 41
US Embassy, Aleje Ujazdowskle 29-31, Warsaw, Poland. Tel: 28 30 41
US Embassy, Neustaedtische Kirchstrasse 4-5, East Germany. Tel: 220 2741
US Embassy, 1 A. Stamboliski Boulevard, Sofia, Bulgaria. Tel: 884 801

Tourist Offices

(USSR) Intourist, 292 Regent Street, London W1. Tel: 01 631 1252
(Czechoslovakia) Cedok, 17/18 Old Bond Street, London W1. Tel: 01 629 6058
(Poland) Polorbis Travel, 82 Mortimer Street, London W1. Tel: 01 580 1704
(Bulgaria) Bulgarian National Tourist Office, 18 Princes Street, London W1. Tel: 01 499 6988

12 SPAIN

Spain is probably the most popular holiday destination with the British and is certainly used to women — from the Club 18-30 brigades to the senior citizens who come to soak up the sun of the Costas. What many travellers, British or otherwise, don't realise is how diverse the country really is, from the forest-clad Pyrenees to the parched La Mancha.

Regional differences are marvellous for the tourist but have caused internal troubles with sections of the country fighting for local autonomy. As you will be aware, of late, some have become increasingly loud in their demands. Galicia, Cataluña and the Basque country of Pais Vasco, for example, all have distinct languages of their own and are extremely separatist.

Moving towards democracy has been difficult for Spain as witnessed by the attempted military coup of 1981, because the country has resisted change. Yet there have been changes. Not so long ago a woman would have been sent to gaol for wearing a bikini, let alone going topless. Less than two decades ago, Torremolinos was a small fishing village not the towering cement resort it is today.

Spain's islands have changed as well. The once sleepy Balearics and Canaries are these days top of the package tour lists.

The Male Attitude

One can't help but think of the typical Spanish waiter. Indeed, according to one Majorca hotel there is a heavy rush for these jobs at the start of the season. Apparently the horde of young English girls who descend on the island is worth the low salary!

A single woman anywhere in Spain can expect plenty of male attention if she's sunbathing by herself or is in a nightclub alone, but it's mostly of the flattering kind and she has but to accept as much as she cares to.

The Spanish are a fiercely proud people, in some cases most arrogant. They are emotional with a love of pageantry and ritual. But they don't have any sense of time. 'Spanish time' is a phrase coined because an appointment for 8 p.m. invariably means 9 p.m. and no apologies. No hour is too late for the Spaniard who, having siesta-ed in the afternoon, revels away half the night.

Where to Stay

Spanish hotels vary considerably since package tours have encouraged a building boom often lacking in quality. There are opulent ones like the quietly aristocratic Ritz Madrid, or the Villa Magna in the same city. There are countless small privately owned hotels and there are those set up by the Spanish government such as the *albergues* which are functionally comfortable and cater principally to the motorist. The other governmental chain is the *paradores*, often converted from historic castles or convents. Their settings are excellent and their room and board rates not expensive. They are so popular that reservations should be made well in advance. Two Spanish hotel chains with a good reputation are Sol and Melia.

Holiday apartments and villas — for rental or purchase — are ubiquitous these days along the coastal areas and in the islands. Most of them are admirably equipped, often part of a complex that has pools, shops, restaurants, sport facilities and sometimes a marina.

The government runs Spanish campgrounds. If you're planning this type of accommodation, pick a Class 1 site.

Getting Around on Your Own

In many cases, a hired car is almost an essential because places of interest are scattered and public transport unreliable. There are good roads certainly, around the major cities and along the coast, but there are also some exceptionally bad roads so be warned.

The national railway system, RENFE, is an alternative, though not one of Europe's best. The most efficient trains are the *Talgo* and *Ter* but a supplement is required for travel on these. Neither the *expresso* or *rapido* are as fast as their names suggest and you'd be best off skipping the *tranvia*, *correo* and *ferobus*.

By comparison, Spain's bus network is good with luxury coaches operating on major routes. They run more frequently and are far cheaper than train travel.

Madrid has its own metro system along with buses and more comfortable micro buses. Buses and mini buses operate in Seville; metro and buses in Barcelona.

Hitching is okay providing you have the time to spend — you know what they say about *mañana* — and providing you can cope with the odd hand on your knee.

Eating and Drinking Solo

Even the dingiest bar or restaurant can prove a lovely surprise so don't be put off by outside appearance. What looks rough and uninviting may well turn out to be a family-run café specialising in local cuisine which you won't find in an international tourist hotel.

Practically every restaurant, regardless of size, offers a *menu del dia* or *de la casa* or *menu turistico*, for a fixed price. And practically every bar serves light snacks as well as drinks — toasted sandwiches are a favourite. *Tapas* bars are recommended for singles, too. *Tapas*, like *mezze*, are a selection of tidbits to hold off starvation until dinner (dinner is always eaten late). Such bars are great places to meet people — there are no worries about being seen in them. Best area in Madrid to look for them are the side streets ribboning off Plaza Mayor. Late night bar hopping you should know is a far more social than drunken exercise.

Look out for a *hosteria* sign — it signifies a rustic, local speciality restaurant in an area of touristic interest. Many of Spain's speciality dishes are known throughout the world, to such an extent that finding an excellent *paella* or *gazpacho* in Spain is sometimes difficult. Don't expect excellence in the package holiday hotels — look to the old quarters of towns.

You can rarely go wrong with *vino de la casa* if only for price — often it's cheaper than coffee, but there are also some very fine *Riojas*.

Since censorship has been flung to the wind, Spanish nightlife offers all. You're cautioned to ask for recommendations in large cities.

The Safety Factor

Admittedly there has been an increase in terrorism in Spain and a few brawls in the downmarket resorts but safety is no more or less than anywhere else. Because the Spanish keep such late hours, wandering about alone at night in central areas of resorts and cities poses no undue problem since everyone else is doing likewise. Main emergency police number is 091.

No-no's

Spain is still Catholic so dress discreetly for church visits.
Avoid cheap bull fights.
Don't drive off into the hills without map, sufficient petrol and bottled water.
Don't be in a rush — ever!

Essentials

Whatever basic or luxury you may need, it's available in Spain's cities, resorts and islands. Obviously, a small tourist centre on a small island like Menorca will only stock limited goods but even one general store manages to carry a variety. Watch out for opening times — most stores close during siesta, sometimes all afternoon, opening again for evening shopping. Large department stores like Corte Ingles and

Galerias Preciados remain open right through the day.

Summer months are very hot in the best known beach spots and cities calling for plenty of sun creams and light clothing. Cities such as Madrid and Barcelona tend to be dressy and you can be as outrageous as you like in Marbella or Ibiza.

Electricity is 110-120v, 50 cycles, though newer buildings have 220v.

Medical Survival

Chemists rotate a 24-hour emergency service so check local papers or ask your hotel concierge. Imported medication is on sale but tends to be expensive and, despite what anyone says, bottled water is desirable.

For medical service in Madrid dial 098; in Palma, Majorca, telephone the Medical Centre 23 00 23 and in Ibiza, dial 30 19 16.

What to do Solo

The heart of *Madrid* is Puerta del Sol and two of the main arteries are Avenida Jose Antonio and Paseo de la Castellana, but there's nothing like sitting in a café in the Plaza Mayor, the liveliest part of town. Go on Sunday and you'll find a stamp market there. The Plaza is close to the Rastro flea market, crowded with people and junk.

Some of the best bars or *mesones* are located in the vicinity, often with live music. Traditional ones are to be found between Plaza Mayor and Puerta Cerrada, the oldest in the streets around the Rastro. Look also in the narrow streets between Puerta del Sol and Plaza Santa Ana and in the popular Malasaña district around Glorieta de Bilbao and Plaza Dos de Mayo where tea rooms, jazz cafés and pubs vie for patronage. Weekends are the liveliest at any of them. Don't hesitate to seek one of Madrid's old established cafés — Café Comercial is one of the most nostalgic and Café Gijon one of the most famous.

Spain's capital is an elegant city with an elegant park, the Retiro, in the middle of it. Two of the main city sights are the Prado, one of the continent's most beautiful art galleries rich with Spanish masters — and the Palacio Real, best seen by guided tour.

An excursion to *Toledo* is highly recommended. Once there, explore on foot the museums and churches of this walled city that was El Greco's home. All the souvenir shops sell the swords, knives and damascene giftware for which Toledo is famous.

Top Basque resort is *San Sebastian* whose old quarter is located beneath Monte Urgull and its more modern section centres around Avenida de Espana. The beach apart, take the funicular up Monte Igueldo for the view; eat down at the port; or see a pelota match.

Most of *Seville* covers the east bank of the River Guadalquivir. The most pleasant places to walk are the Maria Louisa Park and the Paseo de Catalina de Ribera. The main street, Queip de Llano, is where you'll find the cathedral and Giralda Tower. Seville is where you should try Andalusian cuisine and see flamenco.

Granada is most noted for the Alhambra where some people like to spend hours by themselves. A comprehensive ticket admits you to its Casa Real and the extensive gardens. The cathedral houses the tombs of Ferdinand and Isabella in its Royal Chapel and you could take a bus from beside this building to the Arab quarter of Albaicin; but it is not advised to visit Granada's discothèques alone.

Las Ramblas is the central thoroughfare of *Barcelona*, a broad handsome boulevard stretching between the port and the centre of town. Along it are cafés and markets and undoubtedly several street musicians. The showy part of the city is the Ensanche but the most fascinating is the Gothic quarter or Barrio Gotico. However, don't go there at night — it's the worst part of town for crime. Barcelona is most noted for Catalan Gaudi's architecture and its host of museums. Best view is from the Montjuich, reached via funicular.

You may well be familiar with that string of seaside resorts comprising the Costas — Brava, Blanca, del Sol. They are all well developed and are heavily patronised by single people, as indeed are the islands. *The* place to stroll in Palma, *Majorca* is along The Borne. The wealthiest area is the maze of streets in the Portella quarter around the cathedral and palace with nightspots around Plaza Gomilia. Those of you who don't like knees-up resorts like Magaluf and Palma Nova might well prefer Formentor or Deya.

In *Ibiza* it is Ibiza Town which has character and atmosphere, not to mention the best restaurants, but San Antonio is a major beach resort. Unless you're looking for a quiet time, don't go to *Menorca* which is peaceful but rather lonely.

Of the Canaries, we think *Tenerife* is best for solo travellers. Puerto de la Cruz is its liveliest resort — for the beaches head south.

VISA Visas and Inoculations

Visa — none required.
Inoculations — none required.

Useful Addresses

Embassies
British Embassy, Fernando el Santo 16, Madrid. Tel: 419 15 28
US Embassy, Serrano 75, Madrid. Tel: 276 34 00

Tourist Offices
Spanish National Tourist Office, 57/58 St James's Street, London SW1. Tel: 01 499 0901
Spanish National Tourist Office, 665 5th Avenue, New York, NY 10020. Tel: (212) 759 8822

13 SWITZERLAND

Swiss watches ... Swiss bank accounts ... Swiss cheese. They're the things we associate with this small, peaceful, industrious and stable country — and they sum it up. Precision ... money ... clean milkiness. If there is one country where politics don't get ugly, where the crime rate is not a headline and where safety is practically assured, Switzerland has to be it.

Tourism is a major Swiss industry and has long been so. The nationals are pioneers in the art of hoteliering, their schools producing the crème de la crème of management. In this country a lone woman attracts no undue attention and can go her own way undisturbed. If she is here on business, she will be listened to attentively, judged only by her comments and expertise.

The Swiss are meticulous in their business dealings and immaculate in their dress, expecting you to be as law abiding as they are themselves. Neither violent nor volatile by nature, the Swiss are courteous if not always charming and sometimes blunt.

Three languages, cultures and influences come together in Switzerland: the German, French and Italian. Not unnaturally, the German Swiss tend to be the more precise and their towns the more sedate. High life, however, is not a Swiss forte anywhere, save perhaps the cosmopolitan slopes of St Moritz.

When it comes to de luxe hotels the Swiss have few rivals, for their attitudes towards courtesy, comfort, efficiency and cleanliness are almost unequalled. Many of their hotels are grandly elegant, dowagers in finery summoning whatever a guest needs. It says something that so many Swiss establishments are represented by Leading Hotels which only handles the very best. The woman who likes to be pampered will be so in establishments such as Hotel Quellenhof in Bad Ragaz (Switzerland's top spa and golf hotel); the Three Kings in Basel (long famous); Bellevue Palace in Berne (official residence for visiting dignitaries); Hotel Le Richemond in Geneva (exclusive since 1875); or the famous Lausanne Palace.

Prices are, of course, as grand as these places themselves but even the most modest Swiss hotel or pension is spotless and comfortable.

Getting Around on Your Own

However you choose to travel, problem-free movement is guaranteed and punctuality assured. Swiss rail services are some of the finest with a network that covers all principal cities plus small local lines, mountain railways and even steam trains. Best tourist investment is a Swiss Holiday Card which grants unlimited travel over the entire system plus use of the postal bus routes, for specific periods of time at a vastly reduced cost. Other regional runabout tickets are also available — information can be obtained from local tourist offices.

Those postal buses provide an alternative, but equally effective, mode of transport. The system is actually integrated with railway and lake steamer services and runs year round. Driving is eased by good roads and motorways but care is needed through major mountain passes.

Eating and Drinking Solo

Restaurants are of high standard with accordingly high prices, though a service charge is included so tipping is not such a necessity. The Alpine and lake regions are well suited to picnics and there's no shortage of places in which to buy picnic foods.

Terrace cafés and *stuben* (wine taverns), tea shops and panoramic restaurants are all plentiful throughout Switzerland and every one will make you feel welcome. In Basel look along the Rheinweg, a riverside esplanade, or in the Gothic old quarter of town; in Geneva, the atmospheric quarter around Place Bourg-de-Four might tempt you; in Zurich, try stylish Bahnhofstrasse.

The Swiss are best noted for their fondues but all types of cheese makes its way into all types of food. Expect some regional variation as relates to German, Italian or French cuisine. Chocolate is undeniably excellent and even Swiss wines aren't too bad.

The Safety Factor

Safe! But just in case, the police emergency number is 117.

No-no's

Don't litter.
Don't camp outside a proper campsite.

Don't ride a bike or moped off the roads.

 **Essentials**

International brands of everything may be found in the city shops. Remember mountain weather is changeable so, whether or not you plan to walk in the mountains, pack walking shoes, sweaters and rainwear. Warm clothing along with the sunglasses is just as necessary for summering in the Jungfrau as ski clothes are in winter.

Electricity is 220v, 50 cycles in most places.

 **Medical Survival**

The *pharmacie* sells medicines, the *droguerie*, toiletries. Imported pharmaceuticals are readily available and many doctors speak English. Swiss health spas are notably good and the water is safe to drink. In Zurich, phone 47 47 00 for emergency medical aid; in Lucerne, tel: 111; and in Geneva, 20 25 11 for referral to a doctor.

 **What to do Solo**

Zurich's most chic restaurants and boutiques are located along Bahnhofstrasse but between this street and the Limmat River is the old quarter's cobbled streets lined with a number of promising retail outlets. This area of medieval houses, gates and fountains is well preserved and best enjoyed by leisurely walking. On the other hand, the frescoed façades of the guild houses are best seen by boat trip along the River Limmat. And between May and October, an old-time tram makes conducted city tours. Lake cruises are another possibility.

One of the best art collections is in the Kunsthaus on Heimplatz whilst the Swiss National Museum is of cultural interest. Lindt's chocolate factory, located just outside Zurich, is open for tours.

Basel straddles the Rhine and can be explored both by foot and boat. Old Basel, between Gerbergasse and Leonhardsgraben, and Oberoi Rheinweg, best known for its wooden houses, are both pleasant areas for strolling. Pleasure boats cruise along the river itself though one of the most panoramic views of the city is from the Wettstein Bridge.

The city's biggest shopping street, Freie Strasse, conveniently leads to a colourful marketplace in front of a sixteenth-century town hall. Another landmark is the cathedral besides the Münsterplatz housing the tomb of Erasmus, amongst others.

Berne, the capital, is full of arcaded streets, towers and fountains. Prime sights are all to be seen within the compact hilly old quarter. From Berne it is easy to reach the Bernese Oberland resorts. *Lucerne* is a starting point for Alpine excursions as you can see by the surrounding mountains reflected in its clear lake. *Interlaken* acts as a mountain gateway with access to Thun and Brienz Lakes to which day trips are run. Summer visitors knowledgeable in German could try to see a performance of Schiller's 'Wilhelm Tell', annually presented in an outdoor amphitheatre.

Of all the Swiss cities, *Geneva* is the liveliest so it is here you'll find the biggest choice of nightclubs, theatres and, in summer, outdoor entertainment. Like so many of its sister cities, it is a place for walkers — along its lakefront, in the old picturesque quarter between St Peter's Cathedral and Place Bourg-de-Four and by its quays.

There's an impressive museum choice: impressionist paintings are featured at Musée d'Art et Histoire plus the Musée du Petit Palais whilst the Institut et Musée Voltaire was that philosopher's home when he resided in exile here. The best jewellery shops (and Geneva is a major watchselling centre) are located along the rue du Rhone, du Marche and rue de la Croix d'Or.

In the highest Alpine regions, skiing is possible year round but the normal season is from December to April at the best known resorts. Of all the mountains, the Matterhorn overlooking noted ski centre, *Zermatt*, is the most memorable. *St Moritz* is a luxury resort for winter sport enthusiasts, summer watersport enthusiasts and is also a spa town.

Visas and Inoculations

Visa — none required.
Inoculations — none required.

Useful Addresses

Embassies
British Embassy, 50 Thunstrasse, Berne 3005. Tel: 44 50 21
US Embassy, 93 Jubilaeumsstrasse, Berne 3005. Tel: 43 70 11

Tourist Offices
Swiss National Tourist Office, Swiss Centre, New Coventry Street, London W1. Tel: 01 734 1921
Swiss Tourist Office, 608 Fifth Avenue, New York, NY 10020. Tel: (212) 757 5944

14 TURKEY

Turkey is one of those countries you can never be truly sure of. Its heart is Middle Eastern yet much of its outlook is European. In other words, it is a two-faced country and a woman alone should take heed of that.

The trouble, as so often has been the case in Middle Eastern areas, is a certain equation of 'modernity' with 'Western' ideas. If the attitudes towards Western culture are mixed, it is because despite a change to a Roman alphabet and an enjoyment by some Turks of capitalistic products and values, Turkey's heritage is Muslim. Mixed feelings no doubt helped to give rise to political ups and downs, even violence, and it is only very recently that the country has been cloaked with fashionability as a holiday destination.

It is not easy for Turkey to rid itself of the dreaded 'Midnight Express' image but the blossoming beach resorts in the south — the Turkish Riviera along the Mediterranean — are helping. There is a gleam in the developer's eye, thanks to visitors in the last couple of years who have 'discovered' that the combination of warm weather, sand and sea, and archaeological sites is actually cheap here.

Between Istanbul, long a group tourist mecca, and the newer resorts, there are traditional villages and yet to be explored areas. Clearly a case of taking care.

The Male Attitude

Though religion and culture may be different, don't think the Turks aren't hospitable — they are, very much so. Like their Middle Eastern cousins, they go out of their way to fuss over you, lay everything on. Invitations issued by families to stay or eat with them show genuine goodwill and refused hospitality is often upsetting to them.

There is a clearly visible class difference between the poverty stricken 'peasantry' and the wealthy educated who speak English and consider themselves European. At the lower end of the social scale where Islamic influences are strongest, women still remain second class citizens though it is fair to say they lead a sheltered existence. It can, therefore, be asking for trouble to accept certain invitations from male strangers and it goes without saying that you should simply ignore any solicitations, comments or suggestions that you may unwittingly be subjected to.

Where to Stay

Luxury hotels are only to be found in the large cities such as Ankara, Istanbul or Izmir (for luxury read Hilton or Sheraton). Only the luxury hotels are generally air conditioned and what might be called an 'expensive' hotel is still modest for comforts by Western standards. Turkish standards are much lower than elsewhere in Europe.

Cheap accommodation is easy to find (Turkey's hotels probably are Europe's cheapest), but those which are clean and safe for you on your own, are not. Forget budget hostelries. Off the tourist track is only for the adventurous. Service, however, is usually willing and makes some amends for shortcomings elsewhere.

Getting Around on Your Own

Very difficult for those lacking stamina. Forget all thoughts of driving any distances greater than from one end of a resort to the other. For one thing, the country is vast; for another, city traffic is chaotic. The accident rate is notably high and hired cars are not always in pristine conditions. (Even a taxi ride is a nightmare.)

Trains are slow and uncomfortable — forget any ideas of travelling second class unless you're a masochist. The only recommendable service is the overnight express from Istanbul to Ankara when you can reserve a couchette.

There is direct bus service between the main cities which is marvellous for the budget — they're cheap — but a pain in the proverbial since no one is really sure whether they'll arrive much earlier than scheduled or much later. For a route like Istanbul-Ankara, you can purchase your seat just before departure, but for less frequent services, you'll need advance reservations.

Shared taxis (dolmus) are probably a better idea. As in Israel, they follow fixed routes between towns, leaving when they are full up but letting you off wherever you wish along the route. City taxi meters are like as not for show and greedy drivers will readily overcharge. To prevent any misunderstandings, fix the fare in advance.

Locals invariably offer hitchhikers a ride from one town to another, but since Turkish women do not travel alone in this way, accept a lift at your own risk.

Eating and Drinking Solo

Though eating places are plentiful in Istanbul, you may feel most at ease in a hotel restaurant if you're completely on your own. Perhaps an exception is the pleasant string of seafood restaurants along the Bosphorus. Young Westerners tend to gather in those places in Sultanahmet if you're seeking English-speaking company.

Cuisine is more familiar than you may have expected, based as it is on recipes common to the Eastern Mediterranean. Shish kebabs and vine leaves stuffed with pine nuts and rice invariably turn up, many dishes are served with yoghurt and desserts are sticky and sweet with honey and nuts. If you're sure you don't easily fall under the table, try the fearsome *raki*, Turkey's national drink — otherwise stick to the local wines.

Along the coasts, Aegean, Turquoise or Marmaris, you won't feel uncomfortable eating alone at one of the al fresco cafés. There's an active nightlife in Kusadasi and Bodrum whose discos blare away until the early hours.

The Safety Factor

Terrible stories have been told by some; others have been delighted by the people's friendliness. Use your head and lock your door are both good rules and keeping a close watch on valuables wherever you are is an obviously valid recommendation. You should undoubtedly exercise more than due caution if making your own way across the country. In case of real trouble, call your consulate. Istanbul's tourist police only handle cases of theft.

No-no's

Be careful travelling alone anywhere other than main tourist areas.
Don't travel alone in Eastern Turkey.
Don't even consider anything to do with the drug scene.
If you're travelling by taxi from Istanbul's airport to the city, buy a ticket first from the airport police. Don't expect the taxi driver to charge you fairly himself.
Don't try sleeping under the stars — anywhere.
Don't be uninhibited in dress.

Essentials

Except for the best restaurants and top hotels it is quite probable you will not find toilet paper in any loo, so carry some with you in your bag. Though regular toiletries are available, specialised needs may not be fulfilled everywhere so travel prepared. In Istanbul, Istiklâl Caddesi is a good shopping street and there are boutiques in Nisantas and Sisli districts. The Grand Bazaar of course sells just about everything in its thousands of tiny shops.

Electricity: 220v, 50 cycles is most usual.

Medical Survival

Hygiene is often lacking in Turkey so make sure you have sufficient medical insurance coverage and take the kaolin and morphine with you. Be wary of public rest room facilities, be careful of where you eat and don't drink the water.

Pharmacies are called *eczane* and in any of them you can look for the sign *nobetci*, giving the address of the nearest one open all night. A good hotel will find you a doctor should you require one and English-speaking doctors are available at several Istanbul hospitals like the American Hospital, tel: 486030.

What to do Solo

To get your bearings, take an organised sightseeing tour of *Istanbul* before you start hassling with the local bus system. Most of the 'sights', markets and interesting old quarters are located on the southern bank of the Golden Horn in part of what is termed the 'European' part of the city. Modern downtown section centres on Taksim Square, embracing Istiklâl Caddesi and Cumhuriyet Caddesi.

A tour will always include a look at St Sophia, an architectural wonder that was once a cathedral, then a mosque and is now a museum. The Blue Mosque with its six minarets is equally impressive. The Topkapi complex has so much you may well want to return for a second visit. Its jewels and gold in the museums are awe inspiring and, if you're lucky, the restored harem quarters may be open.

Of the many museums in Istanbul, try to see the Tiled Pavilion, a section of the Archaeological Museum which itself houses a fine bronze and marble collection. A multitude of mosques, as well as the most famous two, create Istanbul's skyline. Among them, the Beyazit and the Suleymaniye and the Rüstem-Paşa are particularly worth seeing. One of the best city views is from the top of the Galata Tower.

A boat trip up the Bosphorus is a memorable experience. Ferries provide frequent service to Eyüp, a pilgrimage site and also to the Princes Isles where horse-drawn transportation is the only kind available. One of the most recommendable boat rides is on the express, from Pier 4, which reaches the mouth of the Black Sea in less than two hours. Another boat from the same pier takes the route more slowly, stopping at towns on both the Asian and European sides of the Bosphorus Strait.

Suggested base on the Aegean coast is *Izmir*, a rebuilt port. Not far away towards the beach resort of Cesme you can swim at Inciralti. There are several small seafood restaurants on Izmir's own waterfront and lots of cafés and bazaars in *Kusadasi*, an alternative tourist centre. From either one you can visit Ephesus, a marvellously preserved ancient city ruin through whose streets Cleopatra once rode. Three other historic sites accessible to Kusadasi are Priene, famous for its fourth-century example of town planning; Miletus and Didyma (once the site of Apollo's oracle). The whitewashed houses of *Bodrum* make it one of Turkey's prettiest resorts with its own beach, better ones a little further away, an event-filled summer, a market and a castle.

The most newly 'discovered' coastal strip is that between the Bay of Antalya and the Bay of Mersin — known as the Turquoise Coast. *Antalya* here may be new to us but was a Turkish summer resort over 800 years ago. A few miles away is the sandy beach of Lara and further south Turkey's largest beach resort, *Alanya*.

Turkey's capital, *Ankara,* is a wealthy city whose main boulevard is Atatürk Bulvari, and whose oldest district is Ulus, dominated by the citadel. Two suggested visits here: the Museum of Anatolian Civilisations and Ataturk's tomb. (Ataturk was the French-educated Turk responsible for creating the Turkish state after the collapse of the Ottoman Empire in the First World War.)

Visas and Inoculations

Visa — none required.
Inoculations — none compulsory, but cholera, malaria pills, typhoid and polio recommended.

Useful Addresses

Embassies
British Embassy, 46a Sehit Ersan Caddesi, Gaziosnanpasa, Ankara. Tel: 27 43 10
US Embassy, 110 Atatürk Boulvari, Ankara. Tel: 26 54 70

Tourist Offices
Turkish Tourist Office, 170 Piccadilly, London W1. Tel: 01 734 8681
Turkish Tourist Office, 821 United Nations Plaza, New York, NY 10017. Tel: (212) 687 2194

15 UK

A woman's biggest complaint if seeing Great Britain on her own, is usually that no one talks to her. In reality, the British are much better about this than they're given credit. They have been known to smile or nod to strangers on trains, even exchange a word or two in a restaurant, although they're not as gregarious as their American cousins. At least English is spoken which does simplify things for most people.

Being foreign can work in your favour. An English girl seen sitting alone in an English bar or nightclub may be looked at askance, twice, or with some reservations, but should a foreign accent be heard, all is forgiven.

Not that many years ago, Britain's safety factor and stability was one of its biggest plus factors. Unfortunately, a spate of terrorist bombs and an influx of nationalities with different cultural backgrounds, to cities like London, by necessity has created wary attitudes.

Nevertheless, the country is small and varied enough to see and enjoy in a relatively short time; the National Trust does allow you to browse through its superb properties, unhassled; and the bobbies are still helpful and don't carry guns.

The Male Attitude

The British have retained their attitude of fair play perhaps against all odds. They continue to dislike seeing the underdog 'done', indeed to the contrary, they encourage him to win — witness Sir Freddy Laker's meteoric rise in the popularity stakes. What is 'cricket', and what isn't, does not necessarily refer to the favourite summer game!

Britons are well known for their reserve but this should not be confused with unfriendliness and in no way should a conservative approach be thought to hide a prude. As in other countries, you will note regional differences, not only in accent but also in outlook. Northerners tend to be more talkative, curious — downright nosy if you like, whilst southerners consider themselves the most sophisticated. The Irishman's charm and gift of the gab are almost irresistible; the Scots tend to be dour; and the Celtic streak in the Welsh has always set them apart.

UK

Like elsewhere, the provinces are slower to catch on to fads and fashions. To give an example, not so long ago a provincial magazine refused to run a flat sharing article (mixed sexes) because, though the situation has been a matter of financial fact for many years in the capital, it wasn't done in outlying areas.

The British male is unlikely to prove a nuisance. Unlike the Latin lover, you may have to pursue him before he enters the running — but then watch out! Hospitality, though, comes naturally — look at the innumerable small bed and breakfast guest houses and the pubs, both great British institutions. A point for travellers to bear in mind: the English are home lovers and on a holiday (e.g. Christmas), instead of celebrating on the streets, they retreat indoors.

Where to Stay

The choice of accommodation is outstanding (but not necessarily standardised). Naturally, luxury hotels are among the best, in London aiming for the business and independently wealthy market. Few people fault properties like the Connaught or The Dorchester and most of the internationally known chains manage a British property. The British run chain, THF, operates hotels throughout the country but remember these vary — from four poster inns to functional motels and into topline with Grosvenor House in London's Park Lane.

Luxurious (and often historic) country house hotels are British assets and recent years have seen a spate of them throughout the country — some of the best belong to the Prestige consortium. Lower-priced country inns (no, there aren't any in London) are an excellent bet if you use such listings as the BTA Commended ones. Stately homes, too, have sometimes become hotels, often with titled owners to welcome you through their doors.

Bed and breakfast guest houses have long been the world's best. Most traditionally they are found at seaside resorts. Standards are highly variable so stick to those registered with the English Tourist Board. Some farms accept paying guests and these days, in rural areas, a number of self-catering cottages are available. American-style motels are rare and so are American-style resorts — Gleneagles in Scotland is probably the best.

So far as staying alone, the smaller the property the more comfortable you're likely to feel. In a family-run establishment you'll be accepted as one of the family; in a de luxe country hostelry the staff make it their business to ensure you feel at home.

Getting Around on Your Own

Car hire poses no problems providing you remember to drive on the left and watch out for the roundabouts. Touring Britain by car is highly recommended but Americans may have some difficulties

73

getting used to smaller vehicles and narrower roads. Britain's motorways are excellent and these days, well serviced, but if travelling on other roads don't be misled into thinking a short distance will take a short time. British country roads with all their bends are heavy with traffic in summer.

Assuming there are no strikes, travel by train is another good method for getting around. Cut costs by purchasing a Britrail Pass before arriving in Britain or enquire locally about day and other savers. (Passes are available for unlimited travel on London's public transport which can be useful.)

British coach travel is effective, inexpensive and the routes covered, very extensive. A Rapide service is the speediest way of getting from A to B in a well appointed coach but costs a little more than the regular coach service. Many sightseeing excursions for the day or more are offered by several companies.

Buses connect villages and towns in rural areas, connect country buses to city centres. All cities operate a local bus system and London's underground system is a comprehensive one including a route from the airport to city centre.

Eating and Drinking Solo

Despite the hoo hah and training programmes, so far as I'm concerned, the British are still unused to the idea of unescorted women eating alone so restaurant service may not be as good as if you were with a partner — particularly true at night and especially so outside of city centres.

Hotel dining rooms, however, are used to single diners and every city boasts a plethora of fast-food outlets. Cafés vary: in London, a café is probably a sophisticated glitzy place with an overpriced menu but a comforting ambience. In Manchester, it could be the 'egg and chips' truck stop you'd rather not be seen in. Have a good look before you go in and don't be afraid of walking out again if the interior doesn't appeal.

A few years ago discrimination laws were passed in the UK to stop bars and cocktail lounges refusing entry to single women. My favourite story is being refused service in the Churchill Hotel's bar because I wasn't with a man. They can't do that any more, but it's as well to know hotel watering spots, in London at least, do attract high class prostitutes and you may run the risk of being mistaken for one if you're on your own, particularly by Middle Eastern clientele.

Not true, however, of the wine bar, England's answer to the singles bars. There are literally loads of them, many of them sell some kind of light foods, some are chain owned, all to be recommended for meeting people or not, as you wish. Pubs, other than the touristy kind, are a different story. The average pub in any old street with a name you haven't read about, is not the place for a woman on her own. Pubs in the country, on the other hand, have an entirely different atmosphere of well being.

Perhaps you won't feel exactly at ease in a London nightclub, though it won't turn you away. Many singles patronise the discothèques so here you won't feel out of place, but expect the usual pickup scene in London ones like La Valbonne.

The Safety Factor

Dock and obviously seedy areas apart, you'll feel safe enough in Britain and that includes rural and isolated areas. One wouldn't suggest you go gadding about on the moors or through the woods at night, nor any district that has had racial troubles (e.g. Brixton in London), but use your head, keep your cool and you won't run into trouble. In an emergency dial 999.

No-no's

Don't walk through parks or heaths alone late at night.
Don't wear shorts in the City of London — it's frowned upon.
Don't ask for a gin and tonic in a wine bar — they probably don't sell it.
Don't ask for wine in a pub — it's generally lousy.
If you're going to drink alone in a hotel bar, don't dress too provocatively.
Don't confuse a Pimms with a Shirley Temple — the former is alcoholic.
Don't overtip.

Essentials

Goods from around the world are to be found in British shops but unless the law changes only small grocery stores, delicatessens, etc. open on a Sunday and whilst they stock liquor and wine, it may only be purchased during regular licensing hours.

London's main shopping streets are Oxford Street, Regent Street, Bond Street, Knightsbridge and the King's Road. Food and clothing chain stores like Marks & Spencer's or C & A are to be found throughout the country. Always carry an umbrella in England — no one knows when it will rain next.

Electricity: 240v, 50 cycles AC.

Medical Survival

Every town has chemists which fulfil all medicine and prescription needs and a hotel concierge will tell you which ones are open 24 hours. Large hotels have doctors on call, for which you will be charged, but in an emergency, you will be freely treated under the

National Health in the casualty ward of any hospital.

What to do Solo

London's abundance of landmarks and monuments suggests a sightseeing tour as a requisite. Besides the organised ones, an unescorted trip on an open-topped double decker proves an inexpensive way of familiarising yourself, with a map and guide book to hand. The capital is so rich in places to see it's hard to know where to start, from watching the Changing of the Guards at Buckingham Palace to queuing up to view the Crown Jewels in the Tower of London or browsing in any of the famous museums like the Victoria and Albert.

London's markets are time worth spent — the new Covent Garden complex is a fancy one, surrounded by lively pubs and restaurants. Portobello Road's Saturday antique market doesn't promise bargains but it does have a lot of character, whilst Camden Passage market is foremost for antiques and bric-a-brac. For crafts, Camden Lock Market on a weekend bustles with people and brims with wares whilst Dingwall's restaurant belts out pop and rock. Sunday, by the way, is the day to listen to the soap box orators in Hyde Park or peruse the arts that line the park railings in Bayswater Road.

Walking tours take place almost daily, organised by small groups of guides such as Discovering London or London Walks. Often there's a theme to them: Legal London, Charles Dickens' London, etc. Buy the publication 'Time Out' or ask about them at an information centre. The latter will provide you with information for self-guided tours such as The 'Silver Jubilee Walkway' or 'Heritage Walks'.

One of the most pleasant trips is up river. Year round departures from Westminster Pier and Charing Cross Pier take you to the Tower and Greenwich and in summer, scheduled services travel to Kew, Richmond and Hampton Court. Taking a canal cruise is an alternative, from Camden Lock to Little Venice perhaps or from Little Venice to London's Zoo.

Naturally, London prides itself on its theatres and anyone could spend day after day seeing as many plays and musicals as possible. No company needed. Many women's groups go on matinée days. Try not to miss a performance at the Royal Festival Hall or Albert Hall.

Britain may be a relatively compact island but the visitors main mistake is thinking they can see everything: from John 'O Groats to Lands End is further than it seems. After London, the *Cotswolds* is the favourite area and as photogenic as one would think it to be. In Stratford upon Avon, Shakespeare connections are obvious wherever you go (a Trust runs the five Shakespeare houses all of which may be viewed), but other lovely villages in the vicinity, such as Broadway, are worth seeing too.

Historic interest runs throughout Britain though *Stonehenge* is unique and *Bath* one of the most handsome of British spa towns. Of the seaside resorts, *Blackpool* is the brashest and *Bournemouth* and *Torquay* the most elegant. Don't forget the *Channel Islands* are British either, with more favourable weather. It may be cost effective to buy a package once in Britain though individuals can travel there by air or boat.

A weekend in *Edinburgh* or *Dublin* will allow enough time to see the sights but Scotland and Ireland are excellent countries for touring by car and are most notable for their scenery.

Visas and Inoculations

Visa — none required.
Inoculations — none required, unless arriving from an infected area.

Useful Addresses

UK
American Embassy, 24 Grosvenor Square, London W1. Tel: 01 499 9000.
London Visitor & Convention Board offers services at Victoria Station, Heathrow Airport, Selfridges and Harrods' department stores.

US
British Tourist Authority, 40 W 57th Street, New York, NY 10019. Tel: (212) 581 4700.

16 WEST GERMANY AND AUSTRIA

In many ways, Germany and Austria are similar, their histories intertwined as boundaries have been made and changed. They are both used to strong willed, independent women (their own are) in and out of business so the solo traveller will feel quite at home. If there is any main difference it is visible in the major cities: brash Berlin and trade-minded Frankfurt as opposed to dreamy Vienna and Salzburg. In the smaller towns and villages, that word *gemütlichkeit* (a sense of well being) can be applied to both countries.

Austria's regional differences are perhaps not as pronounced as West Germany's. Officially, West Germany is split into ten *lander* or states, but basically there are five regions. The southerners tend to be more easygoing than the northerners, more akin to their Austrian neighbours. When it comes to trade fairs and conferences, Germany operates at its best but Austria has the greater holiday appeal, especially for its superb ski resorts. In both countries you will note regional language differences with city versus country dialects, but a schoolbook knowledge of German is sufficient to get around and in any case many people speak English fluently.

The Male Attitude

A methodical nature and sense of order prevails. The inhabitants of both countries work hard — and play hard. They respect authority but they love letting their hair down at carnival or holiday time. Beer halls and wine taverns may give the impression of rowdy oblivion to everything, but neatness, practicality and hospitality are a traditional way of life.

There is stiff formality and a sense of humour is lacking, particularly in the north of Germany, though the Rhinelanders and Bavarians are gregarious enough and the Viennese have their own sense of fun. As we know, Germans are quick to lose their inhibitions — among the first to find or create nudist beaches, sensationalise stories or offer pornography. On the other hand villagers cling to traditional customs and folklore, frowning on modern day mores. Similarly Austria wears two faces: its commanding imperial one and its shy surrendering one. (As an example of this, many Austrians are actually titled thanks to ancestral lines, but since the Second World War, these are not permitted to be acknowledged — at least, in writing — but verbally the 'peasantry' still knows its place.)

Overall in this part of Europe, attitudes are courteous; hosts and escorts, considerate.

Where to Stay

The business traveller to Germany will find a plethora of modern de luxe hotels bearing international chain names such as Hilton, Sheraton and Intercontinental. Likewise in Austria. Few of Germany's stylish old hotels survived the war but the Kempinski still stands in Berlin and the Frankfurter Hof is an elegant place to stay in Frankfurt. In Vienna, converted palaces like the Hotel Imperial and Palais Schwartzenburg are perfect retreats for a woman with an expense account. Good consortium names to look out for are Steigenburger and Austrian Hotels.

The accommodation choice is very wide in both countries since there are also spa hotels and castle hotels to choose from. Cleanliness is of such utmost importance that even the tiniest *gasthaus* will be well scrubbed and, although simple, more than adequate, which adds up to comfort for the budget traveller as well. *Gasthof* or *gasthaus* are names given to a small guest house or inn in Germany and Austria. Look for the sign reading *Zimmer Frei* (room to let). Rates at a guest house often include continental breakfast as they do at farm houses.

Getting Around on Your Own

Exceptionally trouble-free in Germany where you may expect efficiency. No problems for self-drive car hirers who can be sure of very fine roads including the *autobahnen* (motorways) which are well serviced with accommodation (*rasthaüser* or *autobahn* hotels), restaurants and 24-hour petrol stations. There is no speed limit but 130 km per hour is the recommended average. (On two lane highways, the speed ranges from 100 km to 120 km per hour.) Austria's roads are good, too, and have equally pristine service stations for coffee and/or toilet stops en route. However, winding roads in the Alps add a few hazards, particularly for winter driving, and road tolls can add up.

If you're driving alone in Germany, at least you are assured of free emergency services, if needed, provided by the country's automobile clubs. Since the Strassenwacht patrols operate on all motorways and major roads, you won't be left in trouble for long.

Germany's railway is also exceptionally efficient if expensive — it is one of the best networks in Europe, always up to date. Lufthansa in conjunction with the railway goes so far as to run super-fast express trains between Frankfurt International Airport and airports at Dusseldorf, Cologne and Bonn. Trans Europe Express trains offer first class only and require seat reservations, but there are many inter-city services operating on a two class system. On board service is better than most other countries, with added conveniences such as radio telephones and multilingual secretarial help.

A variety of reduced tourist train fares are available, especially when purchased outside Germany, though a local tourist office will additionally advise on availability of 'runaround' tickets in a specific area. Train travel in Austria can equally be recommended and is indeed perhaps the best way of enjoying the scenery without a hassle, but you may like to note that the Austrian bus service is also efficient, linking almost every village, including those in the Alps.

Boat travel (most notably on the Danube and Rhine) is another safe, worthy consideration for a female visitor.

Eating and Drinking Solo

The most pleasant watering spots for women are undoubtedly the cafes (*konditorei*) and wine taverns (*weinstuben*). Austria's *konditorei* are world famous and you can still find the traditional ones in Vienna where all kinds of people linger over all kinds of coffees enjoying their newspaper or writing a report — quite alone and accepted. Ordering from a tempting selection of pastries in any one of them goes without saying. Any of the outdoor cafés along Kärtnerstrasse, a main Vienna thoroughfare, are suitable but *konditorei* are located throughout this and every city in Austria.

Wine cellars and outdoor/indoor wine or beer gardens are just as numerous in cities and resorts in both countries. One of the largest tourist centres in Austria for wine gardens is Grinzing but Germany's small Rhineland towns like Rüdesheim also brim with places to sample dozens of wine varieties, listen to bands and probably join in an impromptu singalong or polka. German beer halls, too, may look overwhelming to enter alone — they're large and invariably noisy — but you won't be castigated. Holiday groups and family parties all come to them, sit around large tables, introduce themselves and generally indulge in a merry old time. In German conference cities, stick to the 'old quarters' for rustic charm and good atmosphere (e.g. Schwabing in Munich).

Nightspots in obviously notorious areas such as Hamburg's St Pauli are not for the woman on her own unless she's asking for trouble. In some cases, she may even be refused entrance. Austria's nightlife is far less sleazy, ranging from folksy (zither playing) to a night at the opera.

Both German and Austrian food tends to be heavy: lots of würsts (sausages), sauerkraut, schnitzels and potatoes. Order lightly. German beers and white wines are renowned; schnapps often a proffered aperitif.

WEST GERMANY AND AUSTRIA

 ## The Safety Factor

On the whole, both countries are safe for independent travel. Hitch-hiking, for example, is both legal and effective. Tourist offices in local cities, towns and resorts are helpful and informative. Naturally enough, there are quarters in the larger industrial centres to be avoided — the area in Frankfurt between Hauptbahnhof and the city's inner ring has a bad crime image, for instance, and port areas should be avoided at night if unescorted. Single women are also not advised to use city post office telephones at night, say in Berlin. Phone 110 for the police. In Austria, dial 133.

 ## No-no's

Don't hitchhike on *autobahns* — it's illegal.
Unless you're a judo expert or voyeur of what can be 'sick' entertainment, skip the sleazier clubs along Berlin's Kurfürstendamm and Hamburg's Reeperbahn.
Don't go into a restaurant or beer hall without small change — tipping in the toilets is expected and shouting follows non payment. (The charge is usually stipulated.)

 ## Essentials

No problems with finding essential toiletries, beauty salons or clothing in either country. (Clothing is very smart but highly priced especially in Austria.) *Kaufhäuser* (department stores) are found in every large city, often open at 8.30 a.m., but generally closed on weekends. For packing purposes, remember that the lake and mountain areas of both countries may necessitate sweaters and jackets even in summer. For a winter present to yourself, buy Austrian ski wear.

 ## Medical Survival

Pharmacies and drugstores (*apotheken* and *drogereien*) sell many British and American medicines and toiletries and finding an English-speaking doctor is no problem, though medical treatment is expensive. However, for British travellers there is a reciprocal agreement with the UK under EEC regulations to provide emergency help. The medical emergency number to call in Berlin is 31 03 21 and for ambulance or first aid, 3871. Medical emergency number in Austria is 144.

Health spas are a feature of both these countries (more particularly Germany) where treatment includes taking the waters, mud or sulphur baths, inhalations, hydrotherapy, etc. Any town name with *Bad* in it, is a spa — most famous is Baden-Baden.

What to do Solo

Daytime travel on *West Berlin*'s U-Bahn underground system is safe enough for seeing the city's sights. The most beautiful park in the capital is the Tiergarten housing one of Europe's best zoos, whilst the most accessible example of Prussian architecture is Charlottenburg Castle. Two of the best museum complexes are Dahlem with seven museums featuring priceless art, and Charlottenburg whose Egyptian collection is a focal point. An organised day excursion to East Berlin will show great contrasts.

There are plenty of theatres and concert halls and the city hosts festivals of all kinds. Jazz clubs, pubs and discos are scattered throughout — one of the younger areas centres on Savigy-Platz.

Centre of *Munich* is the Marienplatz, a pedestrianised zone with sidewalk cafés. More cafés can be found down elegant Leopoldstrasse along with boutiques. This leads to Schwabing, a recommendable area in the evening. To the east is Englischer Garten, a popular park for Sunday strollers. Munich has many fine museums: the Deutsches set on an island in the Isar concentrates on scientific exhibits; the Alte Pinakothek has splendid picture galleries; the Bayerisches National Museum, crafts; and the Munchner Stadmuseum portrays the brewing industry through the centuries. Liveliest times of year are during *Fasching*, a winter to spring carnival season, and *Oktoberfest* in autumn, an occasion for heavy drinking and revelry.

The business visitor in *Dusseldorf* will find the Königsallee, a beautiful wide boulevard in the heart of town, an excellent street for shopping and open air cafés. Although basically an industrial city, Dusseldorf also boasts gardens and parks, most extensive of which are the Palace Gardens (Hofgarten). The oldest part of town lays around St Lambertus Church and is worth looking at.

A cruise is one of the best ways for single people to see the *Rhine* where the most scenic stretch winds from Koblenz to Rudesheim. Some of German's best farmhouses (catering to guests) and spa resorts are located in the *Black Forest* region.

Vienna's main tourist attractions lie within the Inner Ring so they can be seen on foot. The key sight is the Hofburg or Imperial Palace which also happens to house the Spanish Riding School. It is difficult to obtain tickets to see regular performances of the famous Lippizaner horses but there are shorter rehearsal mini performances.

Vienna's main artery is Kärntnerstrasse but one of Europe's most handsome streets is the Ringstrasse, studded with numerous imposing buildings including the Opera House, art gallery and Museum of Natural History. One of the city's most important museums is the Kunsthistorisches Museum of Fine Arts.

Music lovers certainly won't feel lonely in this city which supports two superb orchestras — the Vienna Philharmonic and the Vienna

Symphony. The Vienna Opera is world renowned as is the Vienna Boys' Choir. Advance bookings are essential for any top musical performance but you'll hear plenty of Strauss waltzes in the parks in summer or at the Vienna Waltz Cafe (a boat permanently moored on the Danube).

Salzburg is another music lover's paradise for its associations with its native son, Mozart. Happily almost everything in this city is within walking distance of the old centre. At the heart is Residenzplatz, with its seventeenth-century palace, just one of many magnificent buildings where guided tours are given. Mozart's birthplace, Geburtshaus, is now a museum and some of his operas are performed by puppets at the Salzburger Marionetten Theater.

Austria's lakes and mountains provide winter and summer pleasures for skiers and walkers. Lakeside and Alpine villages look like toy towns, their rustic inns and restaurants strung with geraniums. Their charm and hospitable welcome is so obvious that no woman could feel threatened in any one of them.

Visas and Inoculations

Visa — none required.
Inoculations — none required.

Useful Addresses

Embassies
British Embassy, Friedrich-Ebert-Allee 727, 5300 Bonn, West Germany. Tel: 23 49 61
British Embassy, Reisnerstrasse 40, 1030 Vienna, Austria. Tel: 73 15 75
US Embassy, Deichmannsaue, 5300 Bonn, West Germany, Tel: 3391
US Embassy, Boltzmanngasse 16, 1090 Vienna, Austria. Tel: 31 55 11

Tourist Offices
German National Tourist Office, 61 Conduit Street, London W1. Tel: 01 734 2600
German Tourist Office, 747 Third Avenue, New York, NY 10017. Tel: (212) 308 3300
Austrian National Tourist Office, 30 St George Street, London W1. Tel: 01 629 0461
Austrian Tourist Office, 500 Fifth Avenue, New York, NY 10010. Tel: (212) 944 6880

17 YUGOSLAVIA

Yugoslavia is a bit of a 'Lone Ranger' out there in the Communist Bloc. It has managed to keep a politically low profile so far as Russia is concerned and has increasingly been doing its own thing like encouraging tourism, with outstretched hands and a welcoming smile, not to mention holiday facilities.

It appears to be far freer than its neighbours and first-time visitors anticipating drabness are always surprised by its colour and vivacity. They are surprised, too, by its contrasts from Alpine valleys to Adriatic coast, from walled cities to islands.

Yugoslavia is not exactly a united country. History's changes to ruling forces and borders has resulted in a country made up of different peoples speaking different languages, a federation of six republics. Zagreb, for example, is in Slovenia; Dubrovnik in Montenegro. The other provinces are: Croatia, Bosnia-Hercegorina, Serbia and Macedonia. There exist both the Roman and Cyrillic alphabets and three major religions and Yugoslavs can be heatedly proud of their provincial affiliation.

The Male Attitude

Whilst the Yugoslavs are exuberant and friendly not to mention passionate, you can't hope to escape bureaucracy. The book of rules is still the book of rules and it is not easy to coax a Slav into deviating from them or showing flexibility. This has its problems when you want to do something they don't want you to.

As in all countries split into republics, attitudes vary regionally. Slovenia, for example (scenically Yugoslavia's Switzerland) is used to tourists especially in winter and, although the republic is rather rural, it is relatively Westernised. It does, after all, border with Italy and Austria and is somewhat influenced by both those temperaments. The Istrian and Dalmatian coasts have been well exposed to foreigners flocking to the crop of hotels and resort complexes in recent years. Zagreb and Belgrade are as citified as one might imagine but the country's most cosmopolitan centre is Dubrovnik. Macedonia, on the other hand, remains quite primitive. The people are poorer than elsewhere and little has been done in the way of touristic development.

Yugoslavs are generously hospitable. They are hearty eaters and drinkers and will be disappointed if you're not the same. The Yugoslav is charming and courteous but he is also a chauvinist and a womaniser, judging and respecting you by the way you judge and respect yourself. He is determinedly perseverant and a decided flirt. Since Yugoslav women rarely travel alone, outside large cities and holiday complexes, you will be considered fair sexual game. Almost contrary to the traditional attitude, topless and nude bathing are legal — an attraction particularly for German and Scandinavian tourists.

Where to Stay

Hotel standards vary greatly, but prices may not always reflect this. Accommodation in a higher category hotel in a less popular place may cost the same as a lower category hotel in a favourite holiday area. Nor are service and food standards up to those in Western European countries. But the only problem a woman is likely to incur is the language for, except in tourist hotels, it may be difficult to find someone who speaks English.

Holiday Inns and Intercontinental do manage properties in Yugoslavia but for the most part large hotels lack grace and design and feature overbearingly enormous dining rooms (probably with those package tours in mind).

You may even prefer a guesthouse for good value, most prevalent in Slovenia and Croatia, or perhaps a farmhouse — some Slovenian ones take guests.

Getting Around on Your Own

Long-distance travel within the country is difficult and at times hair-raising by car. Apart from the Adriatic coastal route and the autoput from Austria, roads can be bad. The accident rate is also high so think twice before hiring wheels.

Train service leaves a lot to be desired as well. Trains tend to travel slowly, often arrive late and sometimes the network doesn't exist at all. Bus service can be even slower but it's inexpensive and it does get there in the end if you can put up with the innumerable rest stops along the way. Buses and trains are terribly crowded because they're cheap; the only real advantage of travelling by them is meeting the people and that you can't fail to do. If the priority is reaching the destination, pay more and fly.

To make your own way along the coast will take stamina and patience. Only a few of the seaside towns are linked by train to the centre of the country and, as pointed out, buses are jammed. The easier method is via coastal steamer which is reasonably comfortable. Ferries do connect the islands with Rijeka, Split, Zadar and Dubrovnik but the schedules can be unreliable. One of the most efficient services is the daily one from Split to Hvar.

Eating and Drinking Solo

Any café or restaurant will welcome the female traveller and many serve drinks only, if you don't wish for a meal. Visiting an actual 'bar' (other than an obviously tourist one) may not appeal especially if you don't feel like knocking back the *slivovitz*, the local plum brandy. For snacks, you'll find kiosks selling *burek* (a meat filled pastry, or sometimes a cheese one). Most towns seem to have a lively quarter for evening dining — in Belgrade it's Skardarska where musicians play inside and out on the cobbled streets, and the atmosphere of this restored artists' haunt is a most congenial one.

Late night problems are unlikely to arise unless you bump into a very drunken Yugoslav. Many restaurants close early by European standards and nightclubs are few and far between. When they do exist, the only entrance restriction is age — 18 — and you should feel perfectly at ease since they are well-controlled by police.

Food has a tendency to be heavy and the meat better prepared than fish. Two national dishes are *cevapcici* (charcoal-grilled minced meat) and *raznjici* (skewered meat). As for the wine — that flows and flows cheaply enough — best from Slovenia which produces Ljutomer, Traminer and Riesling.

The Safety Factor

One good thing about a socialist country is that it is comparatively safe for the visitor. Respect for the law reduces the likelihood of theft or mugging, etc. In any case, Yugoslavs are usually honest so it's very unlikely that personal possessions or money would be stolen from your hotel room.

In most places the emergency police number is 92.

No-no's

Don't allow yourself to be tempted into arguments about the Church or politics.
Don't hang around coastal port towns alone at night.
Don't sleep or camp on beaches — it's illegal and can evoke fines.
Don't hitchhike, especially away from the coast or main cities.
Don't cash more money than you need — Yugoslav banks won't change it back to 'hard' currency.
It might be better to travel in Macedonia with a male escort.
Don't argue with the police — they're unlikely to see your point of view.

 ## Essentials

Yugoslavia's climate is highly variable, which necessitates clothing homework. Temperatures along the Dalmatian coast are higher in winter than the Italian or French Rivieras, for instance, and spring or summer is generally delightful, but inland, summer month heat can be fiery and winters freezingly cold. Remember also that in the mountainous regions warm cover-ups are necessary in summer.

This country's shops are better stocked than those in other socialist countries but not always with the items you want or need. Do take with you all the cosmetics and toiletries you generally use. It will save searching, frustration and money.

Electricity is 220v, 50 cycles.

 ## Medical Survival

Yugoslavia has a reciprocal arrangement with the UK for free medical aid. English-speaking doctors are available — your hotel will locate one. Dial 94 in an emergency. Take your prescription medicines with you.

 ## What to do Solo

Belgrade's main shopping district is Terazje and one of the main museums is the National at the corner of Trg Republike which houses, among other things, interesting Serbian art. If the weather's warm, take a breather in Kalemegdan park. Business visitors should be reminded that the elegant Intercontinental (the best hotel) is some way from the city centre.

Split is a fascinating medieval town to walk around, fitted within the walls of Diocletian's Palace. Where once were palace halls are now streets and what were rooms have become houses as the Underground Halls (a carbon copy of the Palace's original layout) will show you. See Diocletian's Mausoleum and, for a few dinar, climb the cathedral's campanile. Best souvenir at the nearby outdoor market is local embroidery. Ferries leave Split for the islands of Brač, Hvar, Vis, Korčula and Šolta.

Split is located along the Dalmatian coast which possesses numerous seaside resorts and historic towns. The most famous is further south — *Dubrovnik*. Internationally acclaimed as 'The Pearl of the Adriatic', this exquisite walled city can only be walked through. The major points of interest are the Franciscan Monastery and Cloister, the Dominican Cloister and Museum, the Sponza Palace and the Rector's Palace. The main meeting place is the square where everyone rendezvous at the large café, but there are shops and restaurants tucked into Dubrovnik's alleys. A late afternoon stroll along the top of the walls is rewarding, whilst in summer, Dubrovnik is the setting for many outdoor musical events. Most of the hotels and beaches, though, are outside the old town including the luxury holiday village of Sveti Stefan.

Scenic *Lake Bled* in Slovenia is favoured by Britons. The pretty lakeside resort looks across to a tiny island and an old castle which takes a steep walk to reach. Once at the summit, the view (and the al fresco restaurant) prove worth it.

The main islands for holiday destinations are Brač, Hvar, Korčula and Krk.

Visas and Inoculations

Visa — none required for UK residents; required for US residents.
Inoculations — none required.

Useful Addresses

Embassies
British Embassy, General Zdanova 46, Belgrade. Tel: 645 055
US Embassy, Kneza Milosa 50, Belgrade. Tel: 645 655

Tourist Offices
Yugoslavia National Tourist Office, 143 Regent Street, London W1. Tel: 01 734 5243
Yugoslavia Tourist Office, 630 Fifth Avenue, New York, NY 10016. Tel: (212) 757 2801

THE MIDDLE EAST

The lure of the mystical Middle East is undeniable, despite political instability in some countries in the region. Brought up on epics like 'Lawrence of Arabia', it is difficult to resist thoughts of desert and oases, biblical lands whose names are familiar from school books.

In reality, the pampered Western traveller will not find a bed of roses at the other end. The female executive will encounter difficulties and misunderstandings in doing business and in some places may not be allowed to handle negotiations, e.g. Saudi. The lone holidaymaker may encounter other kinds of difficulties: her independence may not be accepted for what it is.

Women of my cognizance who have travelled solo through the Middle East can't praise it highly enough. By acting and dressing with discretion, they have been granted respectful service and attention, ushered to the front of queues. Western women who live there enjoy a stylish life with servants to cut their chores and private clubs to ease the boredom. But the average female will feel flustered and uncomfortable on her own anywhere outside the relative safety of her hotel.

There are superb luxury hotels in the more cosmopolitan cities like Abu Dhabi, Dubai or Amman in Jordan where a regular business clientele flows in and out. There are destinations where no one bar a fool or news reporter would care to go right now: Iran, Iraq, Libya or Beirut. But for the most part, an escorted tour or at the least a fellow traveller are the best advice.

If you plan to go anyway, remember the three elements: hassles, heat and hygiene. Remember also that much of the Middle East is 'dry'.

18 CYPRUS

Although the little island of Cyprus has been divided since 1974, it says something for its people's stamina and perseverance that tourism continues to flourish — most particularly and effectively in Greek Cyprus.

It was the Greek Cypriots who built a new international airport at Larnaca (to replace that in Nicosia); who built up Limmasol into a major beach resort from what was a major industrial centre; who created Ayia Napa as a new beach centre; and who moved well known tavernas and shops to these newly developed areas.

Though Nicosia continues to act as the island's capital, the east of it is ruled by Turkey which has taken over the picturesque coastal resort of Kyrenia and what was the main seaside resort of Famagusta. It is easy enough to fly into the Turkish Republic of Cyprus from Turkish departure points, but takes a lot of red tape to transfer from the Greek republic of Cyprus to the Turkish area.

So far as the Cypriots themselves are concerned, the single woman has no worries about travelling through this island, will be welcomed as she has always been traditionally welcomed. The British in particular have long favoured Cyprus as a holiday destination and many tour operators offer value-for-money package holidays here.

The Male Attitude

The Athenian may consider himself more Greek than the Greek Cypriot but nevertheless, the attitudes are so similar that the foreigner would find it difficult to differentiate. By nature, the Cypriots are a hard-working lot, diligent, optimistic and God-fearing. They can be as passionate and volatile as the Greek temperament dictates, one moment, and as gentle and subdued as lambs the next. The Cypriot male will be direct, chauvinistic, loving and protective — almost simultaneously. He will chat up a blonde foreigner in a discothèque, even be bothersome, if he thinks it will bring some reward, but he bears no malice, holds no dangerous streak.

As a race, the Greek Cypriots are extremely hospitable, ready to offer their last crumb of bread to the stranger at their door or at their table. Should you get lost in the Troodos Mountains everyone will try to help put you on your right way.

Where to Stay

The business visitor to Cyprus will undoubtedly choose the Cyprus Hilton in Nicosia, but a number of good new hotels are located in the beach areas of Ayia Napa and Limassol. There are also smaller, less expensive and just as pleasant hotels in all these areas.

Getting Around on Your Own

Undoubtedly hired car is your best bet and for British travellers, you drive on the left just as you do at home. The main road system is well surfaced though many roads are narrow, and the island is small enough that you are unlikely to run into major problems. As an alternative, buses link main towns or shared taxis (*dolmush*) may be the quicker way to get from A to B.

Eating and Drinking Solo

In any of the resorts these are cafés and tavernas offering simple meals, Greek style. Fish restaurants predominate especially in Ayia Napa and Paphos. Cyprus wines and sherries are well known.

The Safety Factor

Safe enough. Providing you don't try to cross from the Greek to Turkish sector without the proper papers, there are few worries for the single traveller. The emergency number is 999.

No-no's

Be careful where you break plates!
Don't judge travel time by distance.

Essentials

Necessities, often familiar British labels, are for sale in the shops. Dress is casual wherever you stay. Best shops are in Nicosia where good buys may be made on eye glasses as well as lace and table-cloths.

Electricity is 240v, 50 cycles.

CYPRUS

Medical Survival

Most doctors speak English and imported pharmaceuticals are readily and reasonably available.

What to do Solo

Enjoy the beaches and the hotel pools! The only real sightseeing will take you to Paphos to see some very fine mosaics or to Troodos Mountains, highest of which is Mount Olympus (a winter ski centre) for bracing air and spas.

Visas and Inoculations

Visa — none required.
Inoculations — none required.

Useful Addresses

Embassies
British Embassy, Alexandros Pallis Street, Nicosia. Tel: 47 31 31
US Embassy, Dositheou & Therissou Street, Nicosia. Tel: 46 51 51

Tourist Offices
Tourist Offices in Cyprus: 18 Theodotou Street, Nicosia, Tel: 43374; Democratias Square, Larnaca, Tel: 54322; Spyrou Araouzou Street, Limassol, tel: 62676.
Cyprus Tourism Organisation, 213 Regent Street, London W1. Tel: 01 734 9822
Cyprus Tourist Office, 13 E 40th Street, New York, NY 10016. Tel: (212) 686 6016

19 EGYPT

Visiting Egypt alone can be a nightmare as your arrival in Cairo will give warning. It is one of those airports where everyone jostles and the cacophany in and just outside may make you wish you hadn't got off the airplane in the first place. It is noisy, crowded, hot — just like the capital itself — and no doubt at least three porters will fight to carry your one suitcase and all three will claim a tip.

Egypt is very definitely not Europeanised, however many de luxe hotels it boasts (and there are some super ones). The majority of the population are Muslim; the majority of the population is poor. There is dirt and disease; there is begging and pestering. It is quite inescapable. Women on their own will be hassled especially unless they are taken under the wing of an educated family or business partner, in which case they will find themselves well chaperoned and politely looked after.

Baksheesh (small change) is necessary for absolutely everything. There is no such thing as a helping hand without the other being held out for money. The Pyramids guide, the camel driver *et al.* will more than likely give you an unwanted 'touch up' as well as demand a tip for the slightest service and in the most popular tourist areas no doubt will tell you when the tip is not to their liking. Corruption is a way of life in Egypt. Bear in mind that *baksheesh* judiciously spread around can help make inefficiency a little more tenable, turn a bureaucratic 'no' to a 'yes' and pave the way for regal treatment.

The Male Attitude

Tourists (male or female) are descended upon by hordes of beggars and souvenir hawkers whenever they go outside a hotel or step off a tourist bus. Not surprisingly women are most vulnerable to gropers and should be prepared to deal with the situation with a firm hand, react angrily and sometimes shove unwanted attention out of the way. Such situations will not be the most pleasant but they are not dangerous.

The educated Egyptian will prove an interesting and cordial companion but even he will wonder why a respectable lady should venture unescorted into a nightclub so don't be surprised if you're pestered here, too, albeit if at a slightly different level. Don't trust anyone but the hotel concierge or the tourist office to suggest recommended places to go.

Where to Stay

Cairo is a major business destination and its luxury hotels like the palatial Marriott, the Nile and Ramses Hiltons are all splendid retreats from any city squalor. Their guest rooms and services, their choice of restaurants, bars and coffee shops are all of the highest international standard and their ballrooms and function rooms utilised by the local wealthy elite as well as overseas conference delegates. A businesswoman may prefer traditional establishments such as Shepheard's or the Mena House (near the Pyramids) or, depending upon business schedules, can cut down on traffic travel time by staying in the Heliopolis district (a developed commercial centre half-way between the airport and downtown Cairo).

There is a definite shortage of decent inexpensive and medium price range accommodation throughout Egypt and, outside of Cairo, still not enough in any bracket to meet the demand despite some recent additions in Luxor and Aswan, like the ETAP hotels and a new Club Med. Some of the older, faded hotels do have their charm, though, and you won't feel ill at ease in somewhere as gracious as the Winter Palace in Luxor, one of the grand old establishments. Service in such older hotels can also be more attentive even if all the cons are not exactly mod.

These days the choice of 'floating hotels' on the Nile is so great one wonders that the river has room for them all. Sheraton and Hilton were the first international companies to operate vessels that kill several birds with one stone, providing the housing and feeding and one of the best ways to get around.

Getting Around on Your Own

Travelling by luxury tourist boat is the top recommendation for a single woman wishing to cover the touristic triangle though the option is not a cheap one. Most Nile boats operate on a three or four day itinerary cruising between Cairo and Aswan. A trip on one is a holiday package in itself for it includes three daily meals and all sightseeing along route, very much simpler than having to battle for yourself. The experience is unforgettable and the mode of transport allows for comfort plus culture. Once on board, your travel companions will be British and American in the majority, with a smattering of other mixed nationalities. Travellers with a thirst for learning more than is usual about the ancient splendours of Egypt could take a specialised lectured cruise (e.g. Swan Hellenic).

Egyptair holds the monopoly on internal flights but they still lack sufficient planes. An individual may well find it next to impossible to obtain a seat on a flight and could equally find herself off a flight due to overbooking and group travel competition. Late arrivals and departures, and cancellations without explanation are other situations to be wary of.

Train travel within Egypt has vastly improved for the tourist. The luxury train service between Aswan and Cairo, for example, is reasonably costed and caters meals in the privacy of your own compartment.

Cairo buses are cheap but crowded, dirty and often break down. Take a taxi instead. It should be metered but if not, establish the price before climbing in. Hotels' own taxi ranks are reliable and the doorman usually makes a note of the licence plate especially if seeing off a woman alone at night.

Hiring a car is not a good idea. Battered models, frequent breakdowns, few and far between petrol stations, terrible roads are all the possibilities you'd have to face.

Eating and Drinking Solo

Egypt is not a country where you can happen upon a restaurant which not only serves good local cuisine but has good sanitation to boot. Places for cheap food are plentiful including those selling takeaway *felafel* sandwiches, but you could be taking a health risk by using them. If you care to play safe, eat in a hotel restaurant or ask the tourist office for a recommendation.

Remember that officially a Muslim doesn't drink alcohol which isn't to say *you* can't get a drink since the country has come to terms with tourism, knows it needs it and tries hard to fulfil tourists' requirements. Bars, nevertheless, are the privilege of hotels and private clubs. On occasions, you may find a shortage of imported liquors in which case request a local Stella beer or Omar Khayam wine (rough and ready but sufficing at a pinch). Top hotel bars are generally well stocked but prepare for a high tab.

The Safety Factor

Petty crime is the biggest problem for a tourist. Pickpocketing is the worst hazard, particularly in the bazaar or jam-packed buses, so keep your handbag and valuables close to you at all times. Dirty and undesirable looking neighbourhoods may appear unsavoury, but shouldn't necessitate your pressing the panic button. If in trouble, grab a Tourist Police officer — he's the one with a beret and the words 'Tourist Police' written on his armband.

No-no's

Don't go bra-less.
Dress modestly for mosque visits.

Don't accept invitations from strangers.
Don't hitchhike.

 **Essentials**

All the luxury hotels house a drug store but to prevent hunting around, it's best to bring brand-name toiletries and basics with you. You will, however, find a large variety of necessities for sale both in the bazaar and in Cairo's department stores, many of which are located on 26 July Street, Kasr El Nil Street and Talaat Harb Street.

Egypt is sticky in summer and since the sights are the country's major asset, do pack sensible comfortable clothing — shoes which won't give blisters, sun hats and cool travel clothes.

Electricity is 220v, 50 cycles in Cairo, often 110/120v elsewhere.

 **Medical Survival**

Maintaining good health in Egypt is very essential. Don't fall into the Nile for goodness sake — it's full of bacteria. Nor indeed, drink the water — despite what they say. Bottled water such as the reputable Evian is available and you are well advised to carry it on long full-day excursions say to the Valley of the Kings or Abu Simbel, when most tourists become quickly parched.

You'll probably be advised to take anti-malarial pills. They are not compulsory but if you're a worrier, take them, they won't hurt. Do bring along anti tummy upset medicine like kaolin and morphine, better yet lomotil (prescription pills) or immodium. Few people escape some form of 'gippy tummy'.

There are doctors who speak English — and a luxury hotel will certainly find you one. For anyone who falls seriously ill, the hospital generally recommended is the Maadi Military in Cairo. Medical insurance coverage is vital.

 **What to do Solo**

The centre of *Cairo* is Tahrir Square. Buses to other cities leave from here (if you can wedge yourself onto one); department stores and the tourist office are situated in the streets radiating from it. And one of the capital's most important places is on it — The Cairo Museum. You don't have to be a museum lover to enjoy this, it is honestly a veritable treasure house but to make the most of it, an informed guide is advisable. The riches of Tutankhamun (more than ever went on tour) are a top attraction, but there are so many items of interest, one visit won't do the museum justice.

The Khan el Khalili Bazaar is the most sprawling, bustling and glittering of Egypt's bazaars (those with a good sense of direction won't get lost). There's a 'street' (covered alley actually) for every type of product, from the array of brasses to golden jewellery, fabrics, spices and regular household goods. Barter like mad.

Providing you don't dress outlandishly, you should be able to wander around Old Cairo peacefully enough. In addition to several Coptic churches and the Coptic Museum, see the Ben Ezra Synagogue.

Buses do run out to the Pyramids at Giza, though a taxi will be more comfortable and an organised tour more helpful. The largest of the three Pyramids here is Cheops where you're allowed to climb up inside to the King's Chamber. A word of warning: the passageway is claustrophobically narrow and suffocatingly hot. What's more, the King's Chamber when reached is disappointingly stark. The effort is worth making (just to say you've done it) — but only once. The Sphinx stands in front of the middle pyramid, Chephren. Visit here and you'll have to fight off the souvenir sellers and camel owners determined you should ride and buy. Best bet is an evening's Son et Lumière performance in English.

With a knowledgeable guide, a trip to Sakkara, a Pharaoh burial ground close to the ancient capital of Egypt (Memphis) is worthwhile to see the Step Pyramid, the world's oldest stone structure of its kind.

Alexandria is the Egyptians' answer to Blackpool — *the* beach resort. Frankly, its beach isn't notable but it does have some historical cachet (founded by Alexander the Great for whom it was named) and wartime associations. It is also reasonably cosmopolitan, lively and safe.

Luxor is considered a high point of any Egyptian tour. You can walk along the waterfront without fear — all the tourists do and all those luxury boats pull in here. Take a horse-drawn carriage to Karnak Temple or Luxor Temple. (The Son et Lumière presentation at the former is better than Cairo's.) Sip an aperitif on the terrace of the Winter Garden Hotel and bargain for scarabs and cotton caftans at the riverfront stalls or the back street bazaars.

Across the river lies the most fascinating part of Luxor — the Valley of the Kings, Queens and Nobles (i.e. City of the Dead), whose tombs still bear amazingly coloured pictures and hieroglyphics. These are best seen on a guided tour.

Aswan is a more relaxing destination: the most pleasant way to spend an afternoon is to sail on a *felucca*. Organised excursions are available to Elephantine Island, the Monastery of Saint Simion and Philae Island. From Aswan, it is also possible to take a day trip to Abu Simbel, one of Egypt's most famous temples built by Ramses II.

Visas and Inoculations

Visa — required.
Inoculations — none compulsory, but cholera, malaria pills, typhoid and polio recommended.

Useful Addresses

Embassies

British Embassy, 2 Ahmed Raghab Street, Garden City, Cairo. Tel: 20850

US Embassy, 5 Latin America Street, Garden City, Cairo. Tel: 355 7371

Tourist Offices

Egypt State Tourist Office, 168 Piccadilly, London W1. Tel: 01 493 5282

Egyptian Tourist Office, 630 Fifth Avenue, New York, NY 10020. Tel. (212) 246 6960

20 ISRAEL

Of all the countries in the Middle East, Israel allows the solo woman traveller the most freedom. The people themselves are used to living on military alert but see no reason to let this interfere with tourism in any way — even during the 1983 Israel/Lebanon period of conflict, everyday life continued in its usual way and sunbathers were still enjoying the magic of Eilat.

The country is an old hand at seeing women of all ages on their own. Youngsters, in particular, arrive to stay at the kibbutzim, take a working holiday and hitchhike throughout Israel. Nobody turns a hair. After all, Israeli women themselves are fiercely independent and aggressive. Having said that, a chauvinistic attitude still prevails deep down so that a woman travelling here on business purposes may meet with less success and not such quick acceptance as in continental Europe.

The Male Attitude

It is very much a case of 'real men don't eat quiche' and 'macho is as macho does' which is often translated as 'see how many birds I can pull'. And clichéd as it sounds, dark Israelis do have a penchant for blondes. Blonde or not, if you're alone, you can anticipate being approached on the beach or in the local disco. Israelis are 'Latin' types with something of a raw view of sex, who will determinedly exert both charm and pressure. If you're not in the market, you'll have to be firm to the point of rudeness. However, since Israeli men are also a pretty moral lot underneath (just think of the Jewish family), they are unlikely to appreciate the foreign female of loose morals and once you have won their respect, they are most protective.

Don't forget that Israel also has an Arab population and the Arab culture is more restrictive about dress and behaviour, something lone hitchhikers should bear in mind. In other ways, Israeli and Arab attitudes are similar: generous hospitality for example. You may well find yourself invited into a stranger's home and offered all the food and drink that that household budget can bear. But in Israel, you will be judged by how much you refuse, not how much you accept. Use your own judgement as to where to draw the line.

Israelis, unlike the British, hardly ever call before dropping in. So if you are invited to 'drop in', you can do so without guilt and without phoning first. Life in this country is extremely casual and formalities are somewhat sneered at.

Where to Stay

Israel boasts some very fine hotels in all the major centres, including the newest addition to the luxury scene — The Daniel Hotel and Spa in Herzlia, housing Israel's first complete health and beauty spa (represented in the UK by Leading Hotels, tel: 0800 181 123). The widest accommodation choice is to be found in Tel Aviv and Jerusalem where international chain names like Hilton International and Sheraton have properties. The local recommended hotel chain is The Dan Group.

Several kibbutzim will take paying guests, but don't expect a great degree of comfort at most of them. A full list of available lodgings is available from the Israel National Tourist Office in London, or in New York and/or its offices in Israel.

Getting Around on Your Own

Incredibly easy and cheap — the country is small (just under 35,000 sq. miles) so the distances are short. Buses go everywhere — from town to town and town to desert, mostly run by Egged. (You can buy a card for 25 rides for the cost of 20.) Queuing is not Israeli style so be prepared to elbow! Remember there is no public transport on Shabbat (the Jewish sabbath), from mid-Friday afternoon to Saturday sundown. And if you're planning a fairly lengthy journal, be sure to book in advance and reserve a seat.

Israel's train service is limited so don't rely on it. The best run is Tel Aviv-Haifa and the prettiest, Jerusalem-Haifa.

The most reasonably comfortable and inexpensive way of getting around is by *sherut* (group taxi). They operate between main cities and city and suburbs, leaving as soon as they are full up. You can hail them anywhere along their routes and they'll stop if they have a vacant seat. Sometimes there are fixed schedules (e.g. to Eilat or Jerusalem-Haifa) and then you'll need to book a place.

Hitchhiking is quite acceptable — women and soldiers take priority.

Hiring a car is not recommended. Rental rates and petrol are very expensive and Israeli drivers so manic that unless you feel you can compete, you'll be a lot safer on public transport. (Jaywalking, by the way, can evoke a fine.)

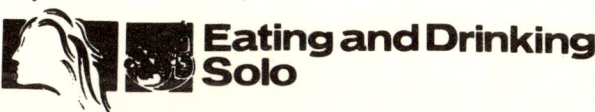
Eating and Drinking Solo

Whether you stay in a five star hotel or a guest house, the only potential worry is being 'chatted up'. Service — to men or women — is not an Israeli forte, but it has improved in recent years. Nor is there a problem when it comes to choosing a restaurant, café or bar, whether it's a smart one along Tel Aviv's Dizengoff Street or a beach-front in Eilat. Just bear in mind that most establishments keep strict Kosher laws with separate meat and dairy sections. That means no milk in your coffee after a meat meal unless you move to the appropriate area. Unlike other Middle Eastern countries, you won't have to worry about hygiene when you wish to buy from roadside food stalls such as those selling *falafel*.

Eating and drinking out isn't cheap, especially for anything imported. In season, locally grown avocados are an excellent buy and Carmel wines are quite palatable. Many locally made soft drinks are available as well as liqueurs — try *Sabra*.

Women are not forbidden entrance to any of the nightspots or discothèques and basically shouldn't feel uncomfortable. Some, though, can be sleazy, including a few in Eilat but more particularly in Judaea and Samaria. Ask your hotel, or indeed any local inhabitant, for a recommendation before choosing on the off chance.

The Safety Factor

Except for obvious no-no's, Israel is a safe country to travel around alone. According to the Israeli Tourist Office, there is no quarter in any city to be avoided. In an emergency dial 100 for the police or 101 for medical emergencies. Any hotel will ring for a doctor for you. Since the country is friendly and convivial, you can almost literally knock on any door for help with any problem.

No-no's

Don't dress indiscreetly when visiting any of the religious sites and most especially in the orthodox Jewish quarters like Me'a She'arim in Jerusalem, where long skirts and long sleeves are expected.
It is asking for trouble to hitch wearing a bra-less top or shortie shorts.
Don't hitch cars bearing a West Bank number plate — you will recognise them by the colour, blue or green. Other number plates are yellow.
Don't walk along the seashore alone at night.
It is ill-advised to go to any of the port areas alone at night.

Essentials

For such a small country, Israel's climate varies considerably. The Dead Sea is very hot in summer; Eilat is perfect in winter; Jerusalem can be quite nippy in January. What is in your favour, though, when it comes to the question of what to pack, is that everywhere is very casual — no dressy clothes will be needed at all.

You will find familiar toiletries readily available in Israel, but they can be rather expensive. Cosmetics certainly are — brand name varieties are gratefully appreciated gifts.

These days, Israeli fashions are worth looking at and there's no problem finding a beauty parlour.

The electricity is 220v, 50 cycles AC.

Medical Survival

Imported pharmaceuticals are expensive. If there's some medication you know you'll need, take enough of it with you. On the other hand, a minor problem that calls for a doctor won't cost you an arm and a leg and, should you have the misfortune to have an accident say in Tel Aviv, you will not be left to die on the streets — you will be carted off immediately to hospital where the care is very good. (The Israeli economy needs tourism and tourists are well favoured when misfortune befalls them.)

Good, English-speaking doctors are readily on call. Local offices of the Israel Medical Association (in Tel Aviv call 256983) will help you find one — so will your embassy. Newspapers list emergency physicians and chemists open at night in main cities. Medical emergency number is 101.

What to do Solo

Since there are plenty of sights in Israel and public transport is safe and efficient, there's no lack of things to do alone even when you choose not to take an organised excursion. *Jaffa*, the old port and Arab quarter of Tel Aviv, for example, is perfectly okay to visit during the day or evening. It has been restored and turned into an artists' quarter where there are cafés, boutiques and art galleries. If you're good at haggling, visit the flea market (Shuq Hapishpishim). *Tel Aviv*'s museums include the Diaspora on the Tel Aviv University Campus in Ramat Aviv, which is particularly thought provoking and well laid out in its coverage of the Jews in exile.

Eilat is such a touristy resort that there's no shortage of people on its beaches, along its promenades and in its cafés. Many shops, fast food outlets and a post office are located near the bus station in the Commercial Center; a series of eating places are to be found down Hatmarim. The number one attraction (and one which needs no human company) is the underwater world. Scuba and snorkel equipment can be rented from the hotels and there are coral reefs worth exploring all along Coral Beach. A must: a look in at the Coral World Underwater Observatory and Aquarium.

Jerusalem to most visitors means the old walled city, most easily entered through Jaffa Gate. It is still laid out in four quarters: Christian, Armenian, Jewish and Muslim though you'll find the whole area Arab influenced. No matter how many expeditions you make here, each will be different and whilst I suggest a first time visitor joins an organised party, thereafter the quarter is best explored by oneself and at leisure. There are eight entrance gates though the Jaffa is the most popular, leading into the most commercial part of the Arab souk, whose main thoroughfare is David Street. The Armenian market centres on Muristan Street and is slightly less overwhelming.

Another good starting point is the Damascus Gate from where you can climb to the walkway along the city walls. St Stephen's Gate leads to the first station of the cross along the Via Dolorosa (the last five are in the Church of the Holy Sepulchre). The other two main shrines are Muslim: the Dome of the Rock and adjacent Mosque o el-Aksa.

For the Jews, the focal point of old Jerusalem is the Western or Wailing Wall where men's and women's sections are separated. It is the remnant of the temple built by Herod and the notes you'll see jammed in between the stones are handwritten entreaties to God by today's Jews — and tourists. This can be reached just inside the Dung Gate.

In New Jerusalem, you can visit the Knesset (parliament) so long as you take along your passport. The Israel Museum here houses an art gallery plus the Dead Sea Scrolls and the Yad Vashem (the memorial museum to the victims of the Holocaust) is a moving experience.

There is a good bus service from Jerusalem to the *Dead Sea*, not only the lowest point in Israel, but in the world. Float in it but don't swim — the salt stings bitterly. There are organised beaches along the coast at Qulya, Ein Freshka, Ein Gedi, Ein Boqeq and Newe Zohar. *Mesada* to the south is one of the great archaeological sites and though there are walking trails to the top, it's far easier by cable car.

Tiberias is the main resort on the Sea of Galilee — very popular with both Israeli and foreign tourists in winter. Take the 45-minute boat trip across Lake Galilee (also called Kineret) for lunch at Ein Gev kibbutz. The speciality is fish and the price is right. Most Tiberias beaches are privately owned and, therefore, charge admission. If you're looking for people and entertainment, try Quiet Beach or Shells Beach and Blue Beach next door, where there are cafés with disco music and evening folk dancing.

VISA Visas and Inoculations

Visa — none required.
Inoculations — none compulsory, but typhoid and polio recommended.

Useful Addresses

Embassies
British Embassy, Hayarkon 192, Tel Aviv. Tel: 249 171
US Embassy, Hayarkon 71, Tel Aviv. Tel: 654 338

Tourist Offices
Israel National Tourist Office, 18 Great Marlborough Street, London W1. Tel: 01 434 3651
Israeli Tourist Office, 350 Fifth Avenue, New York, NY 10018. Tel: (212) 560 0650

AFRICA

If the section on Africa is a little slim it's because there is not much of the continent that is recommendable, save for the most intrepid women. Without any doubts at all, Morocco, Tunisia and Kenya are the three most popular and most easily visited countries for individuals.

But I should point out that Sierra Leone and The Gambia are choice beach destinations for winter holidays although in my opinion, best enjoyed as a twosome. The Gambia, for instance, has superb beaches and hot sunshine, and doesn't take too long or cost too much to reach on a package holiday. Accommodation and sightseeing possibilities are limited, however, and most foodstuffs have to be imported. This is a poor country like so much of the 'Third World', suffering fretful nuisances like a shortage of rental cars, food and drink supplies, maintenance difficulties and mosquitoes. (West Africa is one of the few areas where a yellow fever jab is actually compulsory).

Service is slow in Africa, standards are not always high, and things don't always work. As development goes, most of the continent is only on the first few rungs of the ladder. Having said that, I should also point out that colleagues have convinced me that the Club Med on the Ivory Coast is one of the best, offering superlative food in a superlative setting. And though they're not discussed in detail, the Indian Ocean islands of the Seychelles and Mauritius are long-haul magic. (The latter vary in style: the Seychelles islands are casually informal, often rustic; Mauritius is a more expensive five star island).

As for South Africa, because it's not trouble free at this time, I've left it out perhaps wrongly for, politics apart, this is a majestically beautiful country with a high standard of living; excellent hotels and other facilities; one which speaks English, produces quality wines and other produce. Its transportation system works — its Blue Train is world famous for being a palace on wheels and it offers visitors beaches, game parks, gold and diamond mines, Zulu dancers and ostrich farms. Although omitted here, South Africa's element of danger, so far as foreigners are concerned, is almost exclusive to certain black townships.

21 MOROCCO AND TUNISIA

Because in many ways Morocco and Tunisia are so similar, I have lumped them together for this book's purposes. Basically, they are both Arabic countries but, unlike the Middle East, their beaches and desert sunshine have attracted so many tourists, and urged developers to build more and more resorts, that they are not as worrisome as you might anticipate. This particularly applies to Tunisia, whose women are the most liberated in North Africa.

Thanks to French influences in the past, many Tunisians speak that language, both in the hotels and the bazaars. Morocco, on the other hand, to me, seems more exotic even though these days there are plenty of camp sites and holiday villages along several parts of the Atlantic and Mediterranean coasts, plus luxury hotels in the fine old inland Imperial Cities.

Many single people vacation in both countries which have the best reputation in Africa for warming to their visitors and catering to their tastes without losing their own heritage. These are destinations which you can certainly look favourably upon.

The Male Attitude

Moroccans are a mixture of Arabs, Berbers, Oriental Jews and nomads, somewhat of an eclectic mix. They and their Tunisian neighbours are extremely hospitable (being a good host is *de rigueur*) but they have both been used to 'sheltered' women — many village women still go about veiled — so a Western female should not be too flamboyant.

These are not the only countries to feel that if you're from the West, you're rich, so you can expect money hassles and tipping for everything. Don't be misled into thinking that the well-dressed young Moroccan who professes to be a student wanting to show you a market you'll adore — really is one. He may turn out to be a good guide, but not for nothing. And if it's a special shop he's taking you to, the kickback comes from two places.

Men in both countries have a penchant for blondes, but you can anticipate almost as much sexual harassment even if you're a brunette. In Morocco there will be constant annoyances and do think twice before accepting an invitation from a male stranger. Men of all ages will try to strike up a conversation with you if you sit alone at a café or in a club and it is not likely they are merely being 'just friendly'. You'll have to be brusque about fobbing them off for these are not countries for English politeness.

Hustling is a way of life so you simply must get used to hustling back. In Marrakesh, when I said 'no thank you' to purchasing bead necklaces from a little girl, she tried to fling them at me so I'd have to buy — and I had to fling them back. A 'gift' of a flower is no free gift but a tippable one. Don't accept anything you don't want and make refusals firm. One way to deter hawkers is to offer a ridiculously low price — the hawker is generally so disgusted he'll walk away.

Where to Stay

Skip any kind of budget accommodation that has not been purpose-built for tourists. Luxury hotels in Tunisia are rare but there is plentiful first class accommodation in resort areas like Sousse and Hammamet whose clientele is largely British. Morocco boasts world class hotels like the Rif in Tangier and La Mamounia in Marrakesh as well as lesser rated ones.

Getting Around on Your Own

Not easy, though inexpensive. In Tunisia, trains connect the main cities though their schedules leave a lot to be desired and last minute cancellations are not unheard of.

Driving, yourself, will be a nightmare but you could take a long-distance taxi known as a *louage* which leaves as soon as it is full up with people headed for the same destination. In the cities, make sure you get into a genuine metered taxi as private individuals have a habit of offering 'a taxi' when it isn't one, and then charging the earth for the ride. There are similar problems in Morocco where you can also travel around by train or bus, but unless it is first class, comfort is at a minimum.

Eating and Drinking Solo

In the cities, there are some exceptionally fine restaurants, often geared to business travellers, for which a hotel concierge or holiday company rep will be able to give up-to-date recommendations. There are also places which feature dinner and show (belly dancing, snake charming, etc.), designed to appeal to tourists. Sidewalk cafés in both countries proliferate in all the best known tourist areas and you don't have to worry about sitting at any of them for a cup of espresso or a glass of wine.

Women wishing to save themselves anxiety are best advised not to wander away from the tourist beaten path and should bear in mind that locals often use hotel nightclubs to 'prowl' for female company.

Food is surprisingly good — look out for chicken baked in clay in Tunisia and national Moroccan specialities such as *tajine* (meat with lemon and olives) or *cous-cous* (meat with a semolina base). Plenty of places in both countries sell cheap food but hygiene could be better, so take care. A *brik* (fried egg wrapped in flaky pastry) bought from a Tunisian fast food stand could well be okay, but there's a risk to purchasing food from street stalls in Marrakesh. Wine in both countries is reasonably palatable.

The Safety Factor

Women will feel uncomfortable rather than unsafe in some places, but providing they stick to tourist areas and restaurants; don't commit any no-no's; and dress modestly; the safety factor is fairly good. At any approach of potential trouble, be very noisy. Always watch out for theft especially in the bazaars. If you run into trouble in Tunisia, dial the police emergency number — 197; in Morocco — dial 19.

No-no's

Don't hitchhike.
Don't go bra-less if you don't care to be groped.
Don't buy currency on the black market.
Don't stay in cheap hotels.
Don't wander around after dusk by yourself.
Don't patronise very local-looking cafés and bars where you can't be sure of good hygiene.
Don't walk along beaches at night.

Essentials

Basic essentials can be found in shops in main cities of both countries, including many French brand items, but prices are likely to be higher than at home. Stores tend to close for a lengthy lunch hour/siesta period but reopen later. Laundry service is usually good and not expensive and all good hotels have their own hairdressing salon.

Electricity: in Tunisia, 110-115v, 50 cycles in some places but mostly 220v, 50 cycles; in Morocco, 110-120v, 50 cycles.

Medical Survival

Cleanliness is lacking in both countries (more so in Morocco), so drink only bottled water and avoid salads at anywhere but the best eating places, or fruit that cannot be peeled. Pharmaceuticals are available, often French ones, and there are doctors who speak English or French — the top hotels will find you one if necessary.

The heat can be a knockout. At the height of summer in Marrakesh it may well be around 100°F, so don't try to do too much for too long. High protection sun creams are a must for sunbathing around a hotel pool or on a beach anywhere, even late in the year.

Toilets can be a disaster, often the standup/squat kind and short on air freshener. Avoid all but in tourist hotels or cafés and carry some toilet tissue in your bag.

What to do Solo

Tunis, the Tunisian capital, mixes old with new, Arabic with European. The major thoroughfare is Avenue Bourguiba, reminiscent of a European boulevard. The main attraction is the medina, a marketplace where bargaining is a must — visit during daylight hours. See also the Grande Mosque, but don't wear abbreviated clothing.

A day's sightseeing trip generally takes in Carthage whose ruins are rather disappointing, but also Sidi bou Said, a lovely little white-washed, if over touristy, village where you'll stop for a glass of mint tea.

Hammamet is one of those purpose-built resort areas frequented by Brits. You can walk along the beach to the original village which has its own souk, and just outside it, a 'Western' style shopping centre. *Sousse* is a city cum beach resort, also popular with the British and good for shopping.

Organised sightseeing tours are best to Kairouan, famous for its carpets and the prophet Mohammed's mausoleum. Equally so to the south of the country to the oases of Gafsa, Nefta and Tozuer. Some of the tours include a camel ride in the desert.

Be cautious in *Tangier* — it boasts as many hustlers and thieves as it does tourists and bazaar shopkeepers seem less keen to barter than elsewhere.

Morocco has several what it calls 'Imperial Cities', all worth seeing. In *Meknes*, entered via a monumental gateway (Bab Mansour), there are several sights you can visit on your own. The Tomb of Moulay Ismail, for example, inside a mosque, or the Musee Dar Jamai for its interesting korans. *Fez* used to be one of the country's holiest cities, now with old and new quarters of town. It is worth hiring a guide to tour the Fez Medina and Jewish quarter, or you could get lost.

By comparison to other cities, *Rabat* is very orderly, modern and far cleaner than most. The main road, Avenue Mohammed V stretches right through the medina and ends up at the sea. The best neighbourhood lies between the Chellah (an Arab necropolis built in the ruins of the Roman city, Sale Colonia) and the Hassan Tower. A good view is to be had from Oudaias Kasba fortress in whose gardens you'll find a tea house and the Museum of Moroccan Arts.

The scene at Djemaa el Fna Square in *Marrakesh* is mind-blowing, for it is a day-long, night-long cabaret of story tellers, acrobats, snake charmers, hawkers *et* Moroccan *al*. The most civilised place to watch it all is from the terrace of the large shady café which overlooks the square. Djemaa el Fna borders the massive medina, one of Morocco's most colourful. To see the monuments of the city such as Koutoubia Mosque and the Saadi Tombs, it is best to take a guided tour.

Despite Humphrey Bogart, *Casablanca* is disappointingly industrial and lacking in any of that local colour portrayed in the movie. The tourist area near here is Mohammedia, but stick to the hotel portions of the beach — the locals use much of it to play football on. Most people consider the best beach resort is *Agadir* way down on the Atlantic Coast, with new and modern facilities.

Visas and Inoculations

Visas — none required.
Inoculations — none required, but cholera, malaria pills, typhoid and polio are recommended.

Useful Addresses

Embassies
British Embassy, 17 Blvd de la Tour, Hassan, Rabat, Morocco. Tel: 20905
British Embassy, Place de la Victoire 5, Tunis, Tunisia. Tel: 245 1000
US Embassy, 2 Avenue de Marrakesh, Rabat, Morocco. Tel: 62265
US Embassy, 144 Avenue de la Liberte, Tunis, Tunisia. Tel: 782566

Tourist Offices
Moroccan Tourist Office, 174 Regent Street, London W1. Tel: 01-437 0073
Tunisian National Tourist Office, 7a Stafford Street, London W1. Tel: 01-499 2234
Morocco Tourist Office, 20 East 46th Street, New York, NY 10017. Tel: (212) 557 2520

22 KENYA

Of all the countries in Africa, touristically speaking, Kenya has made the coup. Its hotels are first class, its infrastructure good, its safaris well organised. The coastal strip where sandy beaches, shaded by palm and casuarina trees, border the warm Indian Ocean, is a winter delight to those of us more used to the 'big freeze'. The cooling highlands are rich in vegetation and the relaxed lakelands ideal for bird watching.

There are some parts of Africa which justifiably would fill anyone with trepidation, but not Kenya. It has settled comfortably into independence, always sparing a thought for its holiday visitors.

Perhaps because there are so many mother tongues within Kenya, English has become a common language and is widely spoken by many (the other major language is Swahili). Knowing a little Swahili goes a long way even if it's only a formal greeting — your good mannered attempts will undoubtedly be met by a good natured response.

You could use Kenya simply as a beach holiday in which case all you'd miss is the romantic element, but in my opinion it would be foolish not to incorporate a few days on safari. Safaris are group efforts so you won't exactly be facing that wildlife alone!

The Male Attitude

Many a different tribe has lived, and does live in Kenya including the Bantus and the colourful and terrific-looking Masais who are basically a pastoral people. Most of the Kenyans you're likely to have contact with will be Kikuyu (those outside Kenya say the most intelligent tribe). With few exceptions, all are friendly and, for the most part, helpful. You will also find Arab and Asian elements in the population along with British and other European immigrants.

No woman is likely to meet with trouble unless she disports herself in a fashion that asks for it. Unquestionably, she will be approached if seen sitting alone in a Nairobi hotel or local nightclub but in a beachside resort or safari lodge she probably won't be bothered.

Where to Stay

There are some famous hotels in Kenya like Treetops where Elizabeth first learnt she was Queen and much newer hotels along the coast. Nairobi city hotels include a Hilton and in Mombasa, a good choice of beach hotels including the Mombasa Beach, Serena and Nyali. They're all top flight hotels but not de luxe in the same way as in the Far East — service is not as good and at the Beach you may have the occasional blackout.

Kenya is best known for its lodges. The older ones, when they first opened, were considered incredible oases of comfort, like Kiliguni, in Tsavo West. Nowadays, Taita Hills is the best. Park lodges feature game viewing terraces so you can enjoy the wild without stirring, as game drift to their water holes. On some safaris, tented camp accommodation is provided.

Getting Around on Your Own

The main road from Nairobi to Mombasa is a good enough one to hire a car and drive it. Alternatively, the train offers reasonable service or the trip can be done by air. Getting around the parks on organised safaris is accomplished by mini bus or van.

Eating and Drinking Solo

There are some restaurants in Nairobi like Alan Bobbe's Bistro which may be recommended but frankly you're best off eating and drinking in your own hotel, or another hotel. (The New Stanley's Thorn Tree Café is a well known rendezvous). On safari, you'll be on full board so no decisions need to be made.

The Asian influence has ensured curry is a favourite dish — curry luncheon buffets are a feature at the beach hotels; otherwise, fare is mostly international. Liquor is expensive, wines in particular — beer is the most economical. Kenyan coffee is first class.

The Safety Factor

Yes, Kenya has bank robbers and purse snatchers and Nairobi is not the place to walk around alone at night. Take the usual precautions — don't carry too much cash, lock away valuables. Of the decent citizens I'll say that should your bag be snatched in a Nairobi street, they'll enthusiastically give chase to the thief, like as not beating him up should they catch him before the police.

 ## No-no's

Don't get out of the van in a national park unless told to.
Don't wear inappropriate clothing if visiting a mosque.
Don't rest up at the small garden below Nairobi's International Casino — it's notorious for thieves and con-men.

 ## Essentials

Modern times have brought modern goods to city stores. You may have to pay over the odds for the toothpaste you left behind or the sun cream you ran out of, but you'll find it, though it should go without saying that in the more desolate country areas chances are slim for such purchases. Travel prepared.

Remember that Kenya does have high areas with weather far cooler than at the coast; that it does have a rainy season; and that clothes for safaris need to stand up to heat and dust. Local tailors, by the way, will run you up a safari outfit quite quickly.

Electricity: 240v, 50 cycles.

 ## Medical Survival

If you need a doctor, ask your hotel to help you find one. English-speaking doctors and hospitals are located in Nairobi and Mombasa and it is reassuring to know that a flying doctor service operates to outlying areas.

Tap water is supposedly safe in Nairobi and Mombasa (not elsewhere) but don't take chances. Do not bathe in water upcountry as there's a great risk of bilharzia. Anti-mosquito cream and anti-malaria pills are well advised.

 ## What to do Solo

Nairobi is small enough still to be quite friendly and its centre is easy to walk through during daytime. Stop for lunch in the revolving restaurant of the Conference Centre tower. Browse through the municipal market — the crafts section is at the back. Just bear in mind Kenyatta Avenue is a major central thoroughfare and you can't go too far wrong. One of the standard sightseeing tours from Nairobi takes you to a Masai village where Masai dancers perform and trinkets are for sale, another is to Nairobi National Park.

Mombasa's centre is at the crossroads where Moi Avenue runs into Nkrumah Road and Nyerere Avenue becomes Digo Road. From here you can walk to Fort Jesus, now a national museum, and the harbour with its dhows. This quarter of Mombasa is the oldest, a maze of narrow streets and alleyways. The fish market on the harbour front proves a good subject for budding photographers; shoppers should walk along Biashara Street, or drop in at the municipal market south on Digo Road, for straw goods. The city's most beautiful temple is the Jain.

Although we talk of Mombasa, there are several beaches to the north and south of town which are holiday bases recommended for watersports (the principal ones are Diani, south and Bamburi, north). Much further north, *Malindi* is an important deep sea fishing centre, also with good beaches and accommodation that has increased on recent years. A popular excursion from Malindi is to the island of *Lamu*. The town of Lamu is Muslim with more than 20 mosques. (If you're visiting here, do keep shoulders and legs covered).

Kenya's game parks are renowned the world over and, on a package tour, several might be included. Among the most important are Tsavo West, Amboseli, Meru and the Mara. There's no guarantee that you'll see all of the 'Big Five' (lion, leopard, cheetah, rhino and elephant) but morning and evening game drives should ensure viewing at at least some of them. Best of the lakes are Naivasha and Nkuru whilst Mount Kenya's base is Nyeri.

Visas and Inoculations

Visas — none required, except for UK residents who have previously visited South Africa.
Inoculations — none compulsory but cholera, malaria pills, typhoid and polio recommended.

Useful Addresses

Embassies
British High Commission, Bruce House, Standard Street, Nairobi. Tel: 335944
US Embassy, Moi/Haile Selassie Avenue, POB 30137, Nairobi. Tel: 334141

Tourist Offices
Kenya Tourist Office, 13 New Burlington Street, London W1. Tel: 01-839 4477

ASIA AND THE FAR EAST

Travelling to India and to the Far East is an exciting proposition. The culture, smells, sights and sounds are such a world apart from Europe's that they make the long flight worthwhile.

The complexities — and the structure — of Asia and the Far East have made it impossible to include every single destination in this guide. The likes of Burma, Cambodia, Laos and Vietnam are not really suited to the lone female since they have too many internal problems to work out before they concentrate on tourism with any enthusiasm. Nor have I included the Philippines which currently is trying to pull it all together both domestically and for the holiday market. It is fascinating, but then so is all of the Far East and the islands in the Pacific such as Fiji and Tahiti are undeniably worthy of travel features. But for now, let the chapters on this area of the world hopefully whet your appetite as they are ... the most popular and most easily visited destinations.

Corruption and Oriental/Asian understanding apart, the main problem for a foreign visitor is language communication. One place where you can overcome that is Australia. Although rather further than the Far East, and at the opposite end of the globe, it's well worth the visit, so you'll find a rundown at the end of this section.

23 INDIA

It will move you, horrify you, enthral you and overpower you for India is a giant and complex land. Given that you can stand poverty and dirt thrust under your nose, the pleasures of visiting this country are innumerable. Lately, it has had so much exposure on large and small screen cinema and TV, that more and more people are anxious and able to visit, either with a packaged tour or independently.

There is no way to 'do it all' in one go. After all, India does have miles and miles of scenic sights from its awesome jungles to its highest mountains, plus a bewildering variety of races, religions and customs. But perhaps these contrasts are its greatest attraction.

Do remember that its temperatures are variable, hardly surprising for a land mass that covers 1,261,000 square miles, the world's seventh largest country. And depending upon how and where you wish to travel, the destination can be exorbitantly expensive or incredibly cheap. It is used to solo travellers — it has seen enough of them and it is especially used to youth seeking the mystical.

The Male Attitude

Invariably you will come across a multitude of different attitudes for the people themselves stem from multiple backgrounds. Religion itself gives them argumentative viewpoints: the Brahmins, orthodox; the Muslims whose women stay shrouded; the Hindus and the non-smoking, often bearded Sikhs, the most enterprising businessmen; the emotional Bengalis; the Jains who won't even destroy a fly; and the sadhus, wandering holymen.

In India you may well meet a powerful millionaire; you will certainly pass masses of illiterates. You could well be introduced to a maharajah and never know it since princes these days might be wearing loose cotton costumes or a Savile Row suit. One paradoxical thing is for sure, British visitors receive an especially warm welcome which, considering England was thrown out of India, is totally perplexing but nevertheless a soothing thought.

Indians can be annoying and lovable simultaneously. They are gregarious, convivial, emotional and mercurial. Somehow they manage to be both proud and humble and are almost always indulgent and kind to visiting foreigners. They are good improvisers, take advantage of festivals to party, and are tolerant of what other lesser mortals might consider odd requests or strange whims. You will be well looked after by hosts and well served by guides and hotel staff.

Though times are changing with particular regard to social status and caste system, old habits die hard. Even the educated Indian man who has lived abroad may have his wife chosen for him and be expected to take care of innumerable relations. The traditional respect for women works in your favour and, despite what you may think, Indian women had long ruled the roost before they were allowed to take up careers and earn independent incomes.

Where to Stay

India probably has some of the finest — and some of the worst — hotels to be found anywhere. At the top end are the palaces — real ones like the Lake Palace in Udaipur, converted to a hotel, or the opulent small Shiv Niwas whose surroundings are truly royal. Thanks to a vast labour force who consider service an art, service in all luxury and first class hotels is exceptionally good.

Several of the upper bracket establishments belong to the Taj group, including the Taj Mahal Intercontinental in Bombay and the Taj Palace in New Delhi. Taj is also responsible for some of the best resort properties like Fort Aguada Beach in Goa and Fisherman's Cove at Covelong. Another Indian chain which can certainly take credit for bringing up hotel standards to their current luxury level, is Oberoi — its properties include the Oberoi Intercontinental in New Delhi and the Oberoi Palace in Srinigar.

India's largest hotel chain is Ashok run by the India Tourism Development Corp. and covering all major tourist destinations. Its top properties include the Lalitha Mahal Palace in Mysore and Laxmi Vilas Palace Hotel in Udaipur. Newest luxury chain is The Welcomgroup with hotels that include the Mughal Sheraton in Agra and the Mansingh in Jaipur.

More modest rates are to be found within the Clarks group, usually located in major provincial tourism centres such as Clarks Shiraz in Agra.

Government run guest houses are usually comfortable and inexpensive and a boon in the less well known places. The same goes for the grade 1 Tourist Bungalows which provide private bathrooms and both Western and Indian catering, but second class tourist bungalows are rather basic with variable levels of hygiene. Dak or Traveller's Bungalows and Rest Houses are the most simple. Small cheap guest houses in cities need to be inspected first — some are moderately okay, others you wouldn't be seen dead in.

Getting Around on Your Own

Theoretically this is easy for foreigners who are given priority over everyone else, often allowed concessions on fares and queue jumping for tickets. In practice, trying to arrange your travel movements on your own is a frustrating, sometimes negative experience.

Take Indian Airlines, for example — which you will have to if plans call for a great deal of travel within this sub continent. It may have a computerised system but one which frequently malfunctions and that can cause a great many hiccups. Overbooking, delays, cancellations — be prepared for them all and reconfirm any flight as often as you can!

Train travel is both an experience and a delight — if you have patience. Anyone who watched the television series 'Great Railway Journeys of the World' will realise that planning a lengthy rail trip with connections is not a snap. Low speeds, long distances, not to mention the climate are not perhaps conducive to train travel. However, it can be a fascinating way to see the real India.

Air conditioned expresses operate services between major cities and the accommodation in first class is comfortable. Second class travel on hard crowded wooden seats is a certain way to meet the people but extremely uncomfortable and not to be recommended. One of the famous expresses is the Frontier Mail from Bombay to Amritsar. The day-train, Deccan Queen, from Bombay to Poona is good except for the fact it's not air conditioned. Favourite tourist train is the Taj Express from New Delhi to Agra and the best New Delhi-Bombay train is The Rajdhani. Perfect for touristic touring is a trip on the Palace on Wheels. Inclusive packages over a period of several days are available to Rajasthan from Delhi. You travel in what used to be the private rail coaches of maharajahs, eat on board, sleep on board and take arranged sightseeing side trips.

Rail travel in India is safe and you won't want for food. Even if there's no dining car, all large stations have places which sell refreshments though I have to say the hygiene at some of them is doubtful.

Self-drive cars (even when available) are definitely not recommended but you can hire a car with driver quite reasonably. For getting around Delhi, use taxis — if you find there's an argument over the fare (and there well may be since there are frequent fare increases not shown on the meter plus a rip-off or two), threaten to call the police.

Eating and Drinking Solo

Aficionados of the spicy will find India a food paradise (but remember most Indians themselves are vegetarians). Where you sample that food, however, is sometimes a case of taking your chances. Unless you are given specific recommendations, stick to the restaurants in top hotels — this is not because you're travelling solo but to maintain good health. Luxury hotels can tempt you with regional Indian cuisine and also Western food.

There are so many different types of Indian cuisine, you'll find a lot more dishes than just curry to sample. Spices are the key, of course, even if you can't differentiate between your turmeric and your cardamom, and patrons of Indian restaurants back home will find the familiar birianis, lentil dahl and mulligatawny soups. Breads range from familiar nan and chapattis to those which are deep fried and stuffed, fried with poppy seeds or aniseed. Desserts are often milk based.

Indians are not drinkers — indeed, a number of the populace frown on alcohol which is why it is scarcely available outside of top hotels and tourist restaurants, and even then is extremely expensive. Wines in particular push a budget over the top so bring in as much duty free as you can. Some states are 'dry' but usually hotels are exempted from the no alcohol rule and foreign visitors permitted a special drinker's card. Local gin (thank the British) is fine, whisky is not.

Soft drinks are bountiful though it's best to stick to the bottled variety. If you're buying from a wayside stand, throw away the straw the seller hands you and drink from the bottle having first wiped the rim. As an alternative drink direct from a fresh coconut which will be slashed open in front of you. The Indians drink a good deal of buttermilk, but you can readily order coffee or tea. Do play safe on the water front and ask for bottled (or boiled) and that does mean no ice for the drinks.

The Safety Factor

The sea of faces encountered in every bazaar and city centre, and the mass of beggars who will assail you the moment you leave your hotel, may well seem frightening, but in fact your personal safety is pretty much guaranteed. The biggest problem has to be theft and pilferage including from your hotel room so lock up all valuables. Do carry plenty of small change for tipping ... and tipping ... and tipping, but don't carry it for handouts. Once you give one beggar a coin, you will be assaulted by lord knows how many more. In Delhi the police emergency number is 100.

No-no's

Don't expect vendors and taxi drivers to give you small change back — they may not have it.
Don't expect everyone to accept torn banknotes — annoyingly they won't.
Don't expect to find a swinging nightlife.
Don't photograph people indiscriminately — some don't like it.
Don't wear immodest clothing, most especially to holy shrines.
Don't let your films go through airport X-ray machines unless in a leaded pouch — equipment is often less sophisticated than that which we are used to.
Don't use public toilets outside of hotels (if they exist) or you'll be sorry.

Essentials

Basic necessities are certainly for sale throughout India, but imported brands of toiletries and cosmetics are often unavailable and if they are will cost double. Bring sufficient of your favourite brands with you and if you do have to make such purchases in India, don't expect a wide selection. Hairdressing, on the other hand, is inexpensive though Western hair is better off being handled in hotel salons. Laundry is fast and first rate but, except for the most de luxe of hotels, don't entrust delicate fabrics into a dry cleaner's hands.

Electricity: in most places 220v, 50 cycles.

Medical Survival

All hotels have doctors on call. India is a member of the International Association for Medical Assistance to Travellers (IAMAT) which provides assistance to travellers — with correspondent hospitals in about 15 cities. In Delhi the emergency ambulance number is 102.

There is no difficulty in finding regular medicines, but bring a supply of any necessary prescription ones and if you wear glasses, a spare pair. Basic remedies for stomach upsets like immodium, are a requisite, along with anti-malaria pills, sun barrier and antiseptic creams. Beware of salads and fruit you can't peel and don't buy food from street stalls.

What to do Solo

Old and New *Delhi* have a striking contrast as you move from broad avenues and spacious shopping arcades to a labyrinth of bazaars and small streets studded with monuments. An organised sightseeing tour will show you the Qutb Minar, Humayan's Tomb, the Presidential Palace, Jama Masjid, India's largest mosque and the Red Fort.

Shop in New Delhi around Connaught Place and in Old Delhi around Chandi Chowk. Always bargain hard except in government emporiums. Have your fortune told, listen to sitar music and watch a performance of Indian dance.

In *Agra* spend as much time as you like at the famous Taj Mahal. For all the hot, sticky, jam-packed interior of this famous tomb, it is one of the world's architectural masterpieces. Those who say it's overrated are into sour grapes but it does need time to be appreciated and is probably at its best very early in the morning. Also see the Agra Fort, but don't stop there — take a tour to Fatehpur Sikri, a place which many Agra visitors miss. Deserted these days, it has the advantage of being little changed from the glorious days when it was capital of the Mogul Empire. Agra is famous (when it comes to shopping) for marble inlay work.

Jaipur is one of India's best and prettiest cities — all in pink. Sightseeing here will take you to a quaint observatory, the landmark Palace of the Winds, the City Palace, now a museum, and the Amber Palace. Most romantic Indian city is *Udaipur*, Venice of the East with island palaces and boat tours on the lake. Both cities are located in what to many is India's most colourful province, Rajasthan, whose festival and costumes are of the very stuff you think all of India should be.

Few traditional sights exist in *Bombay* but it is an international gateway to the south. To view it as 'an open air museum' simply stand in Crawford Market where Dadabhoy Naorioji Road meets L. Tilak Road. A horde of small coins pays for a horde of children to carry packages for you (true for other destinations as well). The most fashionable areas are Malabar and Cumballa Hills; the most fashionable promenade, Marine Drive.

For beaches, the recommendation is for Portuguese-influenced *Goa*, the only state which produces any reasonable wine, a state renowned for the hottest of curries, and one of the most relaxed places in the country. Dona Paula is probably the most chic beach and not far from the capital of Panaji. The biggest sightseeing attraction is the Bom Jesus Basilica which contains the relic of St Francis Xavier.

For mountains, who could possibly resist *Kashmir*, truly a jewel in the Indian crown and so very different from anywhere else. It's a sort of Oriental Switzerland, a place through which ancient caravanserai passed on their way to China. The capital, Srinigar, has a bazaar life straight from Arabian nights, is famous for its houseboats and its gardens. Take a shikara ride across Dal Lake, visit Shalimar Bagh and Nishat Bagh gardens, shop for woodcarvings, Kashmir carpets and embroideries.

India's temples are legion and legendary; its bazaars are crammed with tempting merchandise; its folklore splendid. It may be a country which jabbers and gesticulates but it's also an unhurried, timeless country. Give it plenty of time.

Visas and Inoculations

Visas — none required for UK residents; required for US residents.
Inoculations — none compulsory, but cholera, malaria pills, typhoid and polio recommended.

Useful Addresses

Embassies
British Embassy, Chanakyapuri, New Delhi 110001. Tel: 690371
US Embassy, Shantipath, Chanakyapuri, New Delhi 110021. Tel: 600651

Tourist Offices
India Government Tourist Office, 7 Cork Street, London W1. Tel: 01-437 3677
India Tourist Office, 30 Rockefeller Plaza, New York, NY 10020. Tel: (212) 586 4901

24 JAPAN

Japan consists of a chain of islands of which the four main ones are Honshu, Shikoku, Kyushu and Hokkaido. From this distance it appears to be more mysterious and threatening than it is in reality. Much of the country is so Westernised that Tokyo looks like a Far East New York, and in order to show proof of their modernity, the Japanese sometimes forget it is their more traditional elements that are the most appealing.

That is not to say that Mount Fuji has tumbled down or that in season the trees don't drip with cherry blossoms. It is not to say that the art of making tea or arranging flowers aren't still taught. But it is something to bear in mind when planning where to go. And although there are obvious language difficulties, the Japanese for the most part are so considerate and concerned for their foreign visitors, that a woman should not think twice about travelling alone here.

The Male Attitude

The average picture of the Japanese is a band of them, all with cameras strung around their necks, taking so many photographs one wonders what they will do with all the finished results. Outside of Tokyo, it is the same thing — the Japanese like to travel in groups, enjoy taking photos.

They are a curiously (almost overly) polite and courteous nation intent on your well being, which isn't to say they can't be inflexible. The Eastern temperament being what it is makes it difficult for them to give clear cut answers, sometimes frustrating if dealing with an official, and needing specific information.

Like their Chinese neighbours, they cannot bear to lose face and do not like a loss of temper. A smile may well hide anger or any other feeling for that matter, hence the cliché about inscrutability. A Japanese is also easily offended and that can cause bitter resentment. One can often offend without meaning to — if you take a gift to someone's home, for instance, it should always be gift wrapped.

Underneath the cosmopolitan gloss, traditional values are still pretty strong. Family life remains important, conventional dress in cities appreciated. The average man will expect you to be respectable, possibly purposeful and will be helpful, not a hindrance.

# Where to Stay

Japan's luxury hotels qualify as some of the world's best and building continues, adding advanced facilities all the time. You can confidently expect superb service and accommodation in all those hotels of international repute. Indeed, the Japanese themselves are very fond of Western hotels, using them as meeting places for business or pleasure, and for entertaining family, friends or colleagues. Among the best in Tokyo are the Hilton, the Okura, New Otani and Imperial. The capital has grown and spread in such an unplanned way, that your hotel location is less important than its price, for facilities you might want are bound to be scattered in all directions.

To stay in a Ryokan (Japanese inn) is an experience, but an expensive one — sometimes more than a luxury Western hotel, and you will only find them outside of Tokyo. The Ryokan is traditional: paper windows, sliding doors, mat floors for each room in a low building probably with its own garden. You remove your shoes before you go in — and use the slippers the inn provides. On arrival, you'll be welcomed with green tea and left to change into a cotton kimono (also provided). The bath is a deep wooden tub brimming with very hot water in which you sit and relax (actual soaping is done outside the bath). Some Ryokan have public bathrooms à la Roman style. There is no public lounge or restaurant in this type of inn — meals are served in your room by the maid allocated to you. No chairs — just cushions. No bed as we know it, but a futon or floor mattress with a thick quilt. Some concessions have been made to modernity — more door locks and more flush toilets.

Alternative types of accommodation to be found in Japan include what are known as Business Hotels. No, they're not the Hilton variety and there are no services, but they are economical. Minshuku accommodation is a less expensive inn style, like a guest house. You'll have a private room in which to sleep (but no maid service) and will eat with everyone else around a family dining table.

# Getting Around on Your Own

You could drive — there are enough car hire firms — but it is unwise since traffic congestion and unreadable road signs will undoubtedly cause problems. Hiring a chauffeured car is possible but pricey and don't expect the driver to speak English.

Other than air, the most recommendable way of getting around the country is by rail — after all, Japan's trains are famous, most especially the Shinkansen or 'bullet trains', reputed to be the fastest, safest and most punctual of any. So punctual are Japanese trains that when they make a station stop, it's a very brief one so you'd better have your wits about you to get on or off in a hurry. Food is sold on board and telephone calls may be made.

Japan's ferry and steamer service is also extensive. Both cover the

Inland Sea, as does the hydrofoil. Boats may be used as the mode of transport to reach Kyushu, Kobe or Hokkaido from Tokyo and graded accommodation on board includes room with private bathroom.

City public transport is organised and efficient, but crowded and uncomfortable. If you have trouble finding the correct station or buying a ticket, there will always be someone willing to help. If you are using a taxi, have your destination written in Japanese with you, plus directions how to get there if possible. One of the best ways to get around Tokyo is by train (overground and underground). The Yamanote loop line (green) serves the central area; the Chuo line (orange) cuts through the city from east to west.

Eating and Drinking Solo

The choice of where and what to eat is incredible from familiar Western and Japanese fast-food outlets to the more exotic. Some of the finest Japanese cuisine, beautifully presented, is served in a Ryotei which looks like an inn and has a peaceful atmosphere even if its location is in a busy centre. Best enjoyed with an escort.

The Itamae-Ryori will look familiar if you've experienced Japanese restaurants at home. Here, you sit at a counter and watch the chef prepare and cook the food. Sushi (raw fish) bars also feature counter dining or the more squeamish can take themselves off to one of the countless yakitoria (grilled chicken chunks on a stick), tempura bars (deep fried shrimp and vegetables) or teppenyaki houses (broiled steak). It is also perfectly safe to buy bowls of noodles or other foods from street carts. Many what we would call coffee shops show pictures of the dishes they offer so you only need to point to what you want.

Japanese cuisine in its truest form may take some getting used to. Tofu (bean curd) is often presented in a variety of ways and is not to everyone's taste; some of the raw fish (e.g. cuttle) is too rubbery for many; and seaweed wrapped rice may not be what you had in mind. Colour and arrangement is emphasised for every plate.

The national drink is sake rice wine which should be served warm. It is poured into thimble-sized cups or glasses which are so easy to knock back it may be a question of staggering up from the floor at the end of an evening. Japan makes its own reasonable whisky and a few almost palatable wines — beer is the best suggestion.

In Tokyo, one of the most popular evening eating and drinking areas is Shimbashi, but actually each district of the city offers its own selection. Smart young Japan, for example, likes Harajuku district and there are scores of coffee shops, etc. in the Kabukicho area.

The Safety Factor

Japan is one of the world's safest countries with one of the lowest crime rates. By and large the people are honest and if you use ordinary good common sense (i.e. don't walk down dark alleyways), the country should hold no terrors. Obviously take the precautions of leaving valuables in the hotel safe, but a surprising amount of lost property actually finds its way back to its owner. In an emergency, ask someone who speaks English and Japanese to dial 110 for you.

No-no's

Don't wear shorts or beach wear in cities — it's frowned upon.
Don't always tip — it's not always appreciated.
Don't think women-only clubs are lesbian — they are escort clubs with male 'hosts' to dance with or talk, for a fee.
Don't walk alone at night — it's safe enough but you will be looked at askance.

Essentials

You can buy anything you might need in any of the large cities. In addition to speciality shops, there are numerous department stores and supermarkets. Department stores are open on Sundays but closing day during the week varies. Imported beauty preparations are available and used in beauty salons of which there are many good ones in the leading hotels.

Electricity: 100v, 50 cycles.

Medical Survival

Hospitals in Tokyo, Yokohama, Osaka, Kyoto, Kobe, Hiroshima and Okinawa are members of the International Association for Medical Assistance to Travellers (IAMAT) which lists English-speaking doctors trained to British and American standards. If you need a doctor, ask your hotel. The emergency ambulance number is 119.

What to do Solo

The major *Tokyo* sight is the Imperial Palace although this is a new one — the old Meiji Palace was destroyed in 1945. Of the shrines which dot the city, Meiji-jingu is the main one in the centre drawing pilgrims from distant parts. Its wooden *torii* gate is the largest of its kind in Japan. The oldest temple is Asakusa Kannon Temple in the large shopping and entertainment district of Asakusa.

Tokyo is so vast, so crowded, so busy, that at first sight it is a little overpowering. Get it in perspective with an overall view, perhaps from the observation platform of the World Trade Centre, or the Tokyo Tower. On a clear day you could even see as far away as Mount Fuji.

For independent exploration be sure to carry a map. The leading shopping and entertainment quarters are Ginza, Roppongi, Shinjuku Ikebukuro and Shibuya. Do-it-yourself tours might include a visit to the Diet Building and the Parliamentary Museum; a cruise along the Sumida River; or a visit to one of the city's lovely gardens like the highly photogenic Kiyosumi or the huge Shinjuku Gyoen. Several places in Tokyo invite you to watch and take part in a tea ceremony or give lessons in flower arranging. You can try your hand at just about everything here including how to wear a kimono properly — ask where at any tourist information centre (main one at Kotani Building).

Of Tokyo's many amusement centres, the outstanding one is Disneyland! Faithful to the original American concepts with an added Japanese touch. There are day tours here or you can travel independently from Nihonbashi or Otemachi stations to Urayasu, Tozai subway line — a journey which takes about 15 minutes — then the Tokyo Disneyland shuttle bus.

The city's principal museums are located in Ueno Park — the best collections of Japanese art and architecture are in the Tokyo National Museum here.

Shopping can be bewildering so if you're a non-browser, visit the one-shop centres which stock a variety of items including crafts and souvenirs. Using the hotels' own arcades is equally advantageous — no time wasted, no transport worries and counter staff who speak your language. Large one-stop shopping centres include the International Arcade near the Imperial Hotel; the Japan Tax Free Centre, near Hotel Okura; and TOC. The most celebrated shopping district is the Ginza with many department stores in its vicinity such as Mitsukoshi and Takashimaya. You will not be able to barter in Tokyo and other than credit cards the only currency accepted is yen. Look for kimonos, laquerware, ivory and pearls but be careful about selecting antiques (too many forgeries).

The main nightlife areas are Ginza, Shibuya, Shinjuku and Rappongi. You will not be turned away from any nightspot though a Japanese woman would not be seen alone in one. You will feel most comfortable in one of the fashionable discos or at a kabuki theatre.

It is a 300 mile trip to *Kyoto* but its 2,000 plus temples and shrines make it all worth while and the 'bullet train' will make the trip in a mere three hours. Sights to see include the city's largest wooden structure, the sixteenth-century Nishi-Honganji Temple housing several national treasures, the Ginkakuji or Silver Temple and the Kinkajuji Temple or Golden Pavilion. Kyoto is the chief centre for the Japan Noh play but remember a performance can last as long as five hours! It is also a good city for the more traditional arts and crafts.

Nara may be reached from Kyoto on a one day's excursion. Its central landmark is the five-storied pagoda of Kofuku-ji. Foremost sight is Todai-ji (East Great Temple) with its Great Buddha, founded in 745. To appreciate Nara's artworks and culture, a guided tour is recommended.

Visas and Inoculations

Visas — none required.
Inoculations — none compulsory, but typhoid and polio recommended.

Useful Addresses

Embassies
British Embassy, Ichiban-cho, Chiyods-ku, Tokyo 102. Tel: 265 5511
US Embassy, 10-1, Akasaka, 1-chome, Minato-ku, Tokyo. Tel: 583 7141

Tourist Offices
Japan National Tourist Organisation, 167 Regent Street, London W1. Tel: 01-734 9638
Japan Tourist Office, 630 Fifth Avenue, New York, NY 10020. Tel: (212) 757 5640

25 CHINA

Will Hong Kong become more like mainland China or mainland China more like Hong Kong? Invariably, people ask this question and no one right now is too sure of the answer, only that they are slowly moving together.

Up until Beijing opened its doors wide, Hong Kong was a little world on its own, attracting not only business visitors benefiting from its cheap labour, but becoming a major touristic port of call. Numerous women travel here — it's easy to reach by direct (if long) flight and easy to get around. The biggest problem is resisting the temptation to squander money.

Similarly, Singapore has also been a world to itself, a sort of instant Asia with British connections and as much a concrete jungle as New York. Disciplinary measures have made Singapore one of the safest places to be in the East.

Mainland China, on the other hand, is not the easiest place to get around on one's own. It is vast and tourism is new. The language problem is tremendous and the Chinese have a 'group minded' mentality — individuals tend to get lost in the mainstream. But so far as personal safety is concerned, absolutely no worries.

The Male Attitude

The inscrutable face of the East remains inscrutable — one can never be quite sure what the Chinese are thinking. But one thing is for sure, 'keeping face' is most important and 'losing face' the worst possible thing that could happen. For you, this can be frustrating since a Chinese would rather say 'maybe' than 'no' even if 'no' is the final result. An aggressive attitude on your part will not be effective and direct criticism, ridicule or argument are very offensive.

The Chinese do not openly express their feelings so you are unlikely to make an instant friend. In your favour, this same reticence means you will never be pestered. The nearest thing to that is being stared at curiously in the more rural parts of China where 'round eyes' are still a novelty.

Women, of course, are expected to be feminine and retiring, not top-of-the-ladder career women (though Hong Kong Chinese and Singaporeans have learnt to live with this fact). Etiquette (for both sexes) is essential and punctuality expected. The art of compromise and bartering are both ways of daily life and must be carried out with good grace lest face is lost on either side.

Don't forget that most Hong Kong residents are city dwellers but most Chinese are country peasants, so outlooks vary accordingly.

Where to Stay

Both Hong Kong and Singapore can claim some of the world's finest de luxe hotels, made that way by exceptional service and a vast labour force. Both cities can offer literally thousands of air conditioned rooms and suites and many hotels arrange chauffeured service to and from airports. At the present time, Singapore has more luxury rooms than it can sell or fill so can be an extraordinarily value for money buy. Hong Kong hotels, however, are invariably full all year round due to numerous conventions and trade shows held in the colony, so reservations are a must and prices are that much higher.

Luxury Hong Kong accommodation is to be found both on the island, and Kowloon side. Considered crème de la crème are the Mandarin (central, island side) and the Peninsula (Kowloon), both distinguished hotels for discriminating guests. It is difficult to pick the ultimate in Singapore but certainly the Marco Polo, the Pavilion Intercontinental and the Shangri-la are all right up there. In both cities even moderately priced hotels are excellent.

Not so in mainland China. For Western style comforts, the Sheraton Great Wall is hard to beat and The White Swan in Xian is to be recommended. International companies are building hard and fast throughout China (e.g. Hilton in Shanghai) but currently most Chinese hotels leave a lot to be desired. Those in Beijing tend to look like and have the atmosphere of regimental barracks with vast dining rooms (groups, groups and more groups), limited bar stocks and a shortage of English-speaking staff. Nevertheless, they are trying to come up with the services we are used to and one of the Chinese niceties is the flask of hot water (for your tea) placed in every hotel room. It is unwise to stay anywhere but a tourist hotel since, although hygiene and cleanliness have improved in recent years, standards still have a long way to go.

Getting Around on Your Own

Hong Kong taxis are innumerable, metered and reasonably priced. What's more, their drivers know their territory so you should be in good hands. You'll find yellow mini buses operating on set routes, regular bus service on both sides of the harbour and trams on Hong Kong side only.

The fastest way to get around is by underground. It's also the cheapest but try not to use it at rush hour. An alternative way to cross from one side to the other is by ferry which operates frequent service. Ferry travel is also possible to islands like Lantau, departing from the Outlying Island Services Pier on Connaught Road, Hong Kong. Take a rickshaw only if you're a hard bargainer and set the price before you move off. Car hire is not advised — too much traffic, too few parking spots.

Hiring a car in Singapore, on the other hand, is perfectly feasible since traffic moves in a disciplined fashion on the left and street signs are in English. But taxis are cheap enough not to have to bother, or you could splurge on a chauffeured car or budget on a trishaw.

Getting around China itself will undoubtedly mean some flights and is definitely best by organised group. Independent travel by train is fine providing you are assisted in getting the tickets. There are tourist carriages and tourist prices. Trains are comfortable enough though not always to time; the stations, splendidly Victorian. If over-nighting on board, beware the devil radio — you may get an earful of monotonous Chinese music that can't be turned off.

Eating and Drinking Solo

Very much a distinction between those Westernised sections of China and the rest of the country. What is shared is the noise and the somewhat rough decor of any authentic Chinese restaurant. Of course, in Hong Kong and Singapore, there are fancy establishments and such a wide choice of cuisine that whatever your tastes, they'll be catered to. Don't miss at least one meal on a floating restaurant in Hong Kong's Aberdeen and for a good lunch on Causeway Bay, walk down appropriately named Food Street where restaurants and cafés feature all variations of Chinese and Western food.

The main nuisance about eating alone in Hong Kong is not being able to try lots of dishes (unless you leave mounds of food). The most common cuisine is Cantonese which uses plenty of steaming and quick-frying in its preparation. Cantonese lunch (and sometimes breakfast) is *dim sum*, literally snacks in small portions so several types may be ordered. Local liquor and wine tend to be potent and only for aficionados. Best stick to beer like San Miguel.

Singapore is noted for all types of Asian cuisine, not just Chinese and its street markets provide famous (and safe) food experiences. Each hawker has his own territory and his own specialities, so look around first before making a choice which could be *satay* from Malaysia, *murhtaba* from India (pancakes stuffed with meat in a curry sauce) or *hokkien mee*, fried noodles with prawns and pork. One of the best stall food eating places is Newton Circus which sells incredible variations of Asian foods. Another is Rasa Singapura on Tanglin Road or there's the Satay Club down by the harbour and Telok Ayer Market on Shenton Way for Indian or Chinese dishes.

Reports are mixed about the food in the rest of China. Some say they've never had better; others, never worse. It is assuredly different from food served in American or British Chinese restaurants. Like as not you'll end up eating snake or dog whether you know it or not, sea slugs, bean curd and infinite varieties of mushrooms. Cuisine varies regionally: in addition to Cantonese, bread and noodles are emphasised in the north whose famous dish is Peking Duck; Shanghai food is often stewed in soya sauce or fried in sesame oil; Hakka food is simpler like baked chicken in salt; and Szechuan is hot and spicy with plent of chillies.

Chinese tea is nothing like you're used to — the fresh green leaves are used. It may take plenty of practice to drink the tea without swallowing the leaves. Coffee is a rare find and what passes for coffee in some places tastes pretty awful. Bring Nescafé and tea bags with you. Except for breakfast and meals in the best of Westernised hotels, Western food whilst available is not very good.

A word on Chinese nightlife: in Hong Kong, anything suitable for the women alone tends to centre around the hotels. An evening at a Chinese supper club or Chinese opera can be arranged as part of a group. In mainland China, nightlife as we know it doesn't exist and dinner time is around 6 p.m. (Bring books!)

The Safety Factor

It's safe, most especially in Singapore and China proper. Since I can't think readers will be visiting the girlie bars of Hong Kong, that city's only potential problem is pickpocketing. If in real trouble in either Hong Kong or Singapore, dial 999 and ask for police, fire or ambulance. A serious problem in China is best dealt with by the Embassy or tour company rep.

No-no's

Don't automatically think the Chinese like being photographed — some get very angry.
Watch out for religious rulings — to visit some buildings you need to remove your shoes.
Skip the Wanchai and Tsimshatsui areas of Hong Kong unless accompanied.
Don't litter the streets or jay-walk in Singapore, unless you care for a heavy fine.
Don't linger after a Chinese host leaves a banquet — it's impolite.

Essentials

No worries about running short of necessities in Hong Kong or Singapore where shops and markets are arrayed with every conceivable type of merchandise. Made-to-measure clothing as probably everyone knows is one of *the* things you go to Hong Kong for and since both destinations are British, you won't want for familiar brands. For the rest of China take *everything* you think you might need, with you and that includes loo paper, decent soap and shampoo. There are hairdressers but I doubt you'll wish to give one a try.

In Singapore and Hong Kong, electricity is 220v, 50 cycles.

Medical Survival

Medical services as provided in Hong Kong are up to the best standards and any traveller falling sick or suffering injury, will be treated with first class care. Any hotel will call you an English-speaking, accredited doctor or check the local Yellow Pages under 'Physicians and Surgeons'. According to the Hong Kong government, tap water is safe but I wouldn't drink it. In Singapore, it's probably as safe as they say. Here, too, health care is A1. In an emergency, ring the Singapore General Hospital. Mainland China still relies a great deal on herbal medicines to cure lesser ailments and they might just work. If in need of a doctor, speak to a tour guide or rep.

What to do Solo

In *Hong Kong*, take the Peak tram to the top for a panoramic view. Get up early to watch the Chinese do their Tai Chi Chuan exercises (a little like shadow boxing). Take a ride on top of one of the old trams to the end of the line and back again. Visit Ocean Park, the marineland theatre and have your fortune told at the Man Mo Taoist Temple on Hollywood Road.

To absorb all the sights and smells of Kowloon, you really need to stroll around. Just watching the local scenes is sightseeing at its best. Along Saigon Street you'll undoubtedly come across more fortune tellers and street barbers; on Battery Street, paper wares used for burning at funerals; and on Woo Sung Street, stalls selling cooked food, fruit and vegetables.

Take an excursion to Sung Dynasty Village, a recreated ancient Chinese community with interesting cultural and crafts demonstrations. Join a harbour tour — perhaps the Wan Fu owned by the Hilton. Ferry off to Lantau Island where you can escape the bustle and noise.

Shopping need I say requires plenty of time. Bargains are not what they used to be but the glittering piles of goods are a feast for the eyes, and shopping alone is the only way to make careful selection. Don't dismiss the markets where smart buys can be made. You could well find genuine brand labelled clothes at Jardines Bazaar in Causeway Bay and certainly will at Stanley Market (though they may be end of line or seconds). And the Jade Market on Canton Road in Kowloon offers further temptation.

Shopping in *Singapore* also takes time — new facilities seem to be completed all the time. Every hotel has its own, often extensive, arcade. Orchard Road must have at least 12 large complexes. One of the best for value is Peoples Park. Gone are the days when a purchase was 'a steal' but do look in at Change Alley and Raffles Place.

Take a harbour tour from Clifford or World Trade Centre piers. Ferry across to Sentosa Island. Do the tourist 'bit' with dinner at Raffles Hotel followed by the 'Instant Asia' show at the Cultural Theatre. Drop in at Tiger Balm Garden and enjoy the peace and greenery of the botanical gardens.

Highlights in *Beijing* most naturally include a tour of the Forbidden City and a visit to Mao's mausoleum, not to mention the Summer Palace. Shop for embroidered linens and silks in the governmental emporiums and ask about Underground Beijing — the city beneath the city which can be seen by special appointment. All tours go to the Great Wall and include the Ming tombs.

Visas and Inoculations

Visas — required for mainland China.
Inoculations — non compulsory, but for mainland: malaria tablets, typhoid and polio recommended; for Hong Kong: typhoid and polio recommended.

Useful Addresses

Embassies
British Embassy, 11 Guang hua lu, Jian Guo Men Yoi, Beijing. Tel: 52 1961
British Trade Commission, Bank of America Tower, 12 Harcourt Road, Hong Kong. Tel: 230176
British High Commission, Tanglin Road, Singapore 1024. Tel: 639333
US Embassy, Xiu Shui Bei Jie 3, Beijing. Tel: 52 3831
US Consulate, 26 Garden Road, Hong Kong. Tel: 239011
US Embassy, 30 Hill Street, Singapore 0617. Tel: 338 0251

Tourist Offices
China National Tourist Office, 4 Glentworth Street, London NW1. Tel: 01-935 9427
Hong Kong Tourist Association, 125 Pall Mall, London SW1. Tel: 01-930 4775
Singapore High Commission, 2 Wilton Crescent, London SW1. Tel: 01-235 8315
China National Tourist Office, 60E 42nd Street, New York, NY 10165. Tel: (212) 867 0271

26 THAILAND

Most women probably think that Thailand is a 'man's country'. Its image does indeed show countless female attractions and temptations for the visiting male — some of Bangkok's quarters are undeniably notorious. But having said that, the country itself and its people are enchanting (among the most attractive in Asia) and well worth a visit. In the package tour market, Thailand is tops because of this reason and because long-haul prices are almost surprisingly competitive.

The silver screen of the West has helped increase its popularity — who can forget 'The King and I', though you wouldn't find a Thai giving much credence to the story. Rama IV upon whom it was based was a revered ruler who studied Western ways extensively. He was a man with many interests and liberal thought and one who encouraged foreign involvement. Despite reforms, it was however Western ideas which brought an end to the monarchy.

In more recent times, political unrest both within and around Thailand has caused problems yet it has remained relatively stable — hence of great touristic interest — even if the Cambodian capital is only 200 miles away and only the Mekong River separates the country from Laos.

It is a hot humid country requiring physical stamina to enjoy, what with the monsoons from June to November followed once again by a muggy climate. To see the major sights in a short time, it is best visited as part of a tour group.

The Male Attitude

The Thais' traditions and culture are some of the most delightful anywhere in Southeast Asia but old ideas are challenged, and changing at a frightening pace. You'll find the city folk quite materialistic with a penchant for television rather than for more traditional activities and fairs. Like most of the East, slum areas sprawl adjacent to ritzy hotels and office plazas; bartering is mandatory; and backhanders not refused. But the Thais are very polite, softly spoken and well mannered. A willing and graceful people skilled at manoeuvring situations to their own advantage. A Western woman is unlikely to be troubled by a Thai man and will not be made to feel like an outcast even in a girlie club.

Where to Stay

Quality hotels are plush, well serviced and expensive — located naturally in the most popular destinations: Bangkok, the beach resort of Pattaya and Chiang Mai. There is some outstanding luxury accommodation in the capital including a Hyatt, the charming Oriental and the magnificent Peninsular. The Royal Cliff Beach is a large Pattaya luxury hotel but a string of resort hotels cater to the tour group trade here.

A boom in hotel building in the last few years has eased what was a shortage in Bangkok and several of the first class hotels offer such good service and facilities, they could be described as luxurious. Even most in the moderate-price bracket are geared to Western tastes with swimming pools and coffee shops and, naturally, air conditioning.

In the smaller towns, whilst prices are definitely cheaper, Western styles of comfort and food are less available and fewer people speak English.

Getting Around on Your Own

No way by car! Yes, the road network is fine; the drivers are not and insurance coverage isn't compulsory for them. Being involved in an accident in Bangkok is liable to cost you dearly, that's if you can keep your eyes open long enough to face the driving in the first place. Driving might technically be on the left and speed limits 60 km per hour, but few Thai drivers realise either. Leave the international driver's licence at home.

Thailand is a large country so travelling by air may in fact prove most practical, but train travel can be recommended. The trains are clean, comfortable, run reasonably to time and on long-distance routes do provide air conditioned sleeping cars and dining cars. Main services extend from Bangkok. The rail network is also the best way of seeing rural Thailand and its colourful country life.

Buses run everywhere but scheduled tour buses apart, are extremely uncomfortable. Language is often the biggest communication problem and travelling alone is too unnerving but for the most thick-skinned or experienced. You're best off asking a travel agent to direct you to a private luxury bus service if you're headed upcountry.

Much of the local passenger traffic takes to the rivers and canals — and the sightseeing tours using this mode of transport are a great experience. Not such a good idea for simply getting from one point to another.

Within Bangkok itself, taxis are the safest bet for newcomers despite the fact they rarely use their meters. Bargain the fare in advance (with assistance from a hotel doorman). If possible know where you're going or have someone write down in Thai travel instructions — taxi drivers don't have much sense of direction.

Neither do the drivers of three-wheeled samlors, though they're very cheap to use, and fun if you've got the nerve to try.

Eating and Drinking Solo

Bangkok has countless places to eat. If you're already into Thai food — and love it — you're in luck. If unfamiliar, remember that the Thais are addicted to highly spiced dishes, and I do mean highly spiced, so if unaccustomed stick to the touristy restaurants, and watch out for the tiny green and red peppers.

Chillies and coconut are used for many a dish as is lemon grass. Coconut invariably turns up on dessert listings besides in its milky form as with sticky rice and mangoes. The latter grow in abundance, the East's most delicious fruit according to many — the season is March to May. There are all types of bananas and melons and unusual fruits like the rambutan. Wine by the way is fearfully dear so give it up for a spell and bring in all the duty frees you can.

Nightlife is never tame though, as I said earlier, it is more suited to male tastes. A number of nightclubs have pretty hostesses and scantily clad go-go dancers and since there's no lack of local female companionship, you may feel out of place. Only the bravest females venture into the clubs of Patpong Road or the massage parlours.

The Safety Factor

The biggest danger is probably from the traffic — crossing a road can be hazardous let alone riding in one of those trishaw apparatuses. You can and should be on the lookout for pickpockets — very light-fingered — so don't carry valuables, lock them in the hotel safe, and you may as well resign yourself to being ripped off by taxi drivers. In any emergency dial 191 and state simply what you require.

No-no's

Don't throw caution to the wind especially in Pattaya where there have been some security problems like bag snatching.
Watch out for jellyfish at Pattaya but don't fear for sharks.
Don't wear shorts to tour Bangkok's Grand Palace.

Essentials

Although the heat is such to require plenty of changes of clothes, all the good hotels feature same day laundry service. Bangkok's shops stock a wide variety of cosmetics and toiletries including imported ones but the imports are expensive — bring your favourites with you.

You'll never need more than a sweater at the most and should you decide to buy clothing, opt for the beautiful Thai silk, available by yardage or in made up items. Thai cotton is another good buy — Bangkok boutiques sell it in ready-to-wear.

Medical Survival

Insist on boiled water or the bottled variety — don't listen when told tap water is fine. That's as doubtful as buying food from the street stalls. All the top hotels can call you a doctor immediately but the only ambulance services in Bangkok are attached to individual hospitals or clinics.

What to do Solo

Shopping in Thailand is one of the big attractions, but a hint — browse in the vicinity of your hotel first — it's better than sitting in a hot taxi halted by masses of traffic trying to get somewhere else. Neilloware is a popular buy — a type of silver with inlaid designs made into a variety of articles. Semi-precious stones such as zircons are an excellent buy but if you're going to lash out for fine stones, choose a store registered with the Tourist Authority of Thailand, ask for a guarantee — and still bargain like mad.

Bangkok's markets are fascinating if pungent. The well known floating market sadly no longer exists but there are some out of town to be seen on an excursion, like that at Damnoen Saduak. Weekend markets on the outskirts of town offer a fascinating potpourri of merchandise or there's Banrak, off New Road, which converts to an open-air restaurant at night, or Pratunam Market on Rajdamri Road where masses of packed stalls sell all the necessities and non necessities of life. Chinatown, around Yawarad Road, features its own host of interesting shops — look for those selling gold.

One good way to see things on your own without getting lost is to take a waterbus along the Chao Phya River or any of the city's main canals. These services are very cheap to use and depart from a central point next to the Oriental Hotel. Travel for a few miles, get off to explore the riverside streets and return the way you came.

Scattered around Bangkok are hundreds of *wat* (sorts of temples) whose main chapel or *bot* conceals one or more figures of Buddha. One of the most famous is the Emerald Buddha in Wat Phrakaeo in the grounds of the Grand Palace. The Buddha figure is a 31 ft model crafted in green jasper housed in a golden-roofed chapel. In the Palace itself, the Kings of Siam once held court. Close by, the 160 ft Reclining Buddha is another major monument, housed in Wat Po. On the banks of the Chao Phya River stands a particularly striking landmark — Wat Arun or the Temple of the Dawn whilst the most symmetrically beautiful is the white marble Wat Saket, golden spired and sheltering one of Thailand's largest bronze Buddhas in its shrine. One last *wat* not to be missed is that containing the Golden Buddha

— said to be over five tons of solid gold. A guided, organised city sightseeing tour should take in all these landmarks.

Pattaya is the nearest beach resort and one of Asia's largest. It may not be Acapulco exactly, but you'll find that kind of atmosphere here, and certainly less pollution than in the Mediterranean. Indeed, the underwater swimming is good and a full range of watersports is offered by a variety of hotels. Less developed but on its way to bigger and better commercial things, is the island province of *Phuket*, renowned for excellent beaches, scuba diving and boat excursions. Accommodation is still reasonably priced and European food is available. (Many British tour operators include a visit to Phuket).

By way of contrast, *Chiang Mai* is the other most popular destination in Thailand, located in the hills, where the weather is slightly cooler and fresher. Popularity has created a new commercial area outside the city's old walls and touristic development is prevalent, e.g. the opportunity for a 'Kantok' dinner and elaborate cultural shows in 'Old Chiang Mai' cultural centre. Tours can be arranged to see the three most important *wats*: Wat Phra Tat Doi Sutep, Wat Suan Dork and Wat Phra Sing. On a half day excursion you can visit the caves at Chiangdao or the waterfalls of Mae Klang.

Visas and Inoculations

Visas — none required for stays of up to 15 days.
Inoculations — none compulsory, but cholera, malaria pills, typhoid and polio recommended.

Useful Addresses

Embassies
British Embassy, Wireless Road, Bangkok. Tel: 253 0191
US Embassy, 95 Wireless Road, Bangkok. Tel: 252 5040

Tourist Offices
Thailand Tourist Office, 9 Stafford Street, London W1. Tel: 01-499 7679
Thailand Tourist Office, 5 World Trade Center, New York, NY 10048. Tel: (212) 432 0433

27 MALAYSIA

Until rubber became such a sought after commodity, Malaysia was little known and sparsely settled. Even today, the eastern section entices few others than anthropologists studying remote tribes.

Thanks to a very strong British influence, however, there is an alliance, a feeling of familiarity: in clubs established by the British, cricket continues to be played; horse racing egged on by Chinese sporting instincts, plus polo; gin slings and a knowledge of the language; and tropical sunsets.

Most of Malaysia's population is Malay but a large percentage is Chinese and a small percentage, Indian. Much of the country is still jungle which only the intrepid travellers will have a mind to visit. For all that, Malaysia has become a key holiday destination in Southeast Asia, able to boast some of the best beaches to be found anywhere. The country's natural beauty and hospitality are encouraging to tourists and a foreign visitor will feel favoured, not fearing of malice or over-exploitation.

The Male Attitude

The remnants of colonialism may slowly be disappearing and Bahasa Malaysia is the teaching language in schools, but you will find all commercial and civil service contacts speak English. For the most part, the average Malaysian is a delight — entertaining and informal, friendly and helpful. Restrictions thankfully are few and, apart from the usual Eastern frustrations, threatening situations are unlikely.

Where to Stay

Since tourism became important, the hotel scene has altered considerably. The newer hotels are designed to please the most discriminating of guests and are particularly geared to a business clientele in Kuala Lumpur. Hotels are large, offering all necessary facilities and are efficiently run. Because they do provide a resort atmosphere besides, they attract an even broader range of guests. Prices are higher in Kuala Lumpur than elsewhere due to the number of business meetings finding it a valuable location. Among the de luxe hotels in the city are a Hilton, a Regent and a Holiday Inn. Independents on a budget will find adequate surroundings at any Chinese hotel or Government Rest House.

Getting Around on Your Own

Malaysia is probably the only region of Asia where it is safe to tour by self-drive car. There are a wide range of cars for hire through such firms as Avis and Hertz which operate offices in several cities and allow cars to be collected in one place, dropped off in another. Thanks can be given to the British, who, when they withdrew, left Southeast Asia with a first class highway system, one which the Malaysian government has since added to, paving roads into many a remote *kampong* (village).

This is one place where first class travel is not necessary to find decent hotels and food, decent modes of travel. Borneo apart, the Malayan Railways run comfortable trains, mostly air conditioned, most with dining cars and sleepers. Fares are also reasonable and rail passes are available for 10 or 14 days for a fixed price. One of the main routes starts at Singapore heading for Kuala Lumpur.

Long-distance express buses are fine also thanks to the standards of the roads, though seats must be reserved. Luxury tour bus service between Kuala Lumpur, Singapore and Penang is available through Masmara Tours. (Prices include air conditioned transport so necessary in this tropical climate, English-speaking guides and accommodation in first class hotels).

Taxis are plentiful in Malaysian cities. Bargaining undoubtedly will be necessary and sharing with someone else could be most economical. Agree on a fare before getting into a tricycle rickshaw.

Eating and Drinking Solo

Although you may feel more at home in one of your own hotel restaurants, thanks to a high standard of hygiene, you could eat out almost anywhere in the major Malaysian cities and beach resorts. The variety of foods produced by a polyglot society may well encourage the adventurous traveller to sample sanke meat as well as her satay, roasted crabs and Bombay curry. The most popular and inexpensive beverage is a local beer — Tiger or Anchor but there's no shortage of Singapore Slings over the hotel bar.

The Safety Factor

Anyone who isn't a shrinking violet will find Malaysian tourist spots perfectly safe, the people helpful and friendly. We don't suggest you head for isolated mountain areas or interior jungles, but otherwise, no untoward problems should arise. Just think, most phone operators speak English and the emergency number for police, fire or ambulance is that oh-so-familiar UK one — 999.

No-no's

Don't walk alone down dark alleys in Kuala Lumpur.
Don't wear abbreviated clothing to visit mosques, and keep shoulders covered.
Don't necessarily expect to shake hands with a man unless he makes the appropriate gesture first. (Islam is the main religion and social rules are quite strict, especially on the east coast).
Don't dress too elegantly if you visit a nightclub alone — they'll think you're 'available'.

Essentials

British influences will stand you in good stead and there are enough shops around in tourist areas to fulfil most needs. Penang's main shopping centres include Comtar, or take a look along Campbell Street, Bishop Street and Penang Road.

Electricity is 220v, 50 cycles.

Medical Survival

Since Malaysia has one of the highest standards of living in Asia and one of the best health records, medical survival is relatively easy, and hospitals and medical services have a good reputation. Officially, tap water is safe anywhere on mainland Malaysia but bottled water is readily available.

What to do Solo

A sightseeing tour of *Kuala Lumpur* will show you the older side of the city — its Buddhist temple on Jalan Maharajalela; its Chinese temples on Jalan Petaling and the oldest one on Jalan Cheng Lock. Such buildings are in great contrast to the modern skyscraper hotels and parliament buildings. Intrepid shoppers with time to spare could better enjoy browsing and bargaining in the older sections of town rather than the newer centres. Nor should they miss the 'Sunday Market' which actually takes place on a Saturday night in Kampong Bahru.

Most popular destination is *Penang* for its beaches. It has retained its exotic aura whilst becoming more comfortable for visitors thanks to expanded tourist facilities such as hotels and excursion possibilities. Its capital, Georgetown, never ceases to look busy — best way to get around is by trishaw (drivers usually speak English). Stop off at Carnarvon Street for the best of Chinese goods or ride the funicular railway on Penang Hill. The favourite beach is Batu Ferringhi, those beautiful white sand coves on the north end of the island are rather remote.

MALAYSIA

One of Malaysia's prime hill stations is Cameron Highlands, accessible from Kuala Lumpur, a base to explore the mountain trails, highest of which is Mount Brinchang. As befits a highland area, there are tea plantations: regular tours are given through Boh Tea Plantations.

Visas and Inoculations

Visas — none required.
Inoculations — none compulsory, but cholera, malaria pills, typhoid and polio recommended.

Useful Addresses

Embassies
British Embassy, 5 Jalanfemantan, Damansara Heights, Kuala Lumpur 30732. Tel: 254 1533
US Embassy, 376 Jalantunrazak, Kuala Lumpur 50400. Tel: 248 9011

Tourist Offices
Malaysia National Tourist Office, 17 Curzon Street, London W1. Tel: 01-499 7388

28 INDONESIA

Indonesia is a sort of despairing paradise. The thousands of islands which comprise it have great beauty, but travel between them can be frustrating and the poverty overwhelming. True, the economy is blossoming and communications, improving but delays and inconveniences are still pretty much a matter of fact.

The fascination is not only a scenic one. A population that is the eclectic result of many tribal and ethnic groups is naturally one with a multitude of folk customs and traditions. Strange dances and ceremonies are, for the visitor, colourful entertainment. Local festivals take place throughout the islands, some continuing for days at a time.

Apart from the purely physical efforts of travel and the difficulties that incurs, there are relatively few bothers for women other than loneliness. Who, after all, really cares to splurge on a single flight to the magic island of Bali when it is so well known to honeymooners?

Touristically speaking, Indonesia has not been fully explored. Jakarta and the rest of the island of Java are known. (The business capital is also a connecting point for other parts of the Far East and Australia). The large island of Sumatra is often included on group tour itineraries and Bali, as mentioned, is the most popular destination of all.

 The Male Attitude

Indonesia wears so many faces of the East, it is hard to define one overall attitude. A once strong Hindu influence now only exists in Bali, for example, but Chinese and Islamic influences have added to the Indonesian temperament. Most predominant in Javanese, proud and cultivated.

An undeniable gap separates the rich and poor; corruption is expectable. The people are friendly to foreigners even if they quarrel amongst themselves. They are extraordinarily polite and are embarrassingly hospitable to those they like and trust. On the other hand, laziness is a national trait — swift smiles come more quickly than swift service.

Where to Stay

De luxe hotels are extremely costly but necessary unless you feel you can cope staying in an Indonesian boardinghouse known as *losmen*. In Jakarta, especially, accommodation in an air conditioned hotel with swimming pool and other standard luxury hotel features is soothing against the abrasive heat and dust of this frenzied city. All the top chain names manage Jakarta properties: Hilton, Intercontinental, Hyatt and Mandarin.

In Bali, too, hotels are mostly of luxury grade and located close to Denpasar or on Sanur or Kuta beaches. There are, however, some inexpensive guest houses as there are in most Indonesian towns and hill resorts.

Getting Around on Your Own

Apart from Jakarta and Bali, it's a pain. Domestic flights are frequently overbooked or cancelled; trains are limited to Java; and any travel arrangements must be reconfirmed time and time again. Unless you are already travelling on a package organised from Britain, any on-the-spot travel plans or side excursions should be made through a travel agent — Nitour is the oldest, is government-owned and has offices in all major tourist centres.

Since bartering is a way of life be prepared to argue for everything, including car hire and taxis. (Jakarta is the only place with metered taxis). Hard bargaining is equally necessary to hire a bicycle rickshaw which may be available at costs according to distance or by the hour. In any case, you will need to know exactly where you're going.

Eating and Drinking Solo

Most suitable restaurants regretably emphasise international fare though you may be lucky enough to find a good *rijstaffel* (an Indonesian banquet comprising many little dishes of spicy specialities) in one of the hotels. The small eating places in downtown Jakarta and cheap *nasi padang* food shops are not recommended, if only for medical reasons.

Seafood is okay in coastal cities but the favourite delicacy is *saté*, grilled skewered meat served with a peanut sauce. *Gado gado* (a mixture of vegetables with peanut sauce) also frequently appears on menus. Costs on everything, from a pizza to a cocktail, are invariably high.

For music and entertainment, stick to the hotels.

 ## The Safety Factor

Violence against foreigners is rare though pickpocketing is not. Keep a close eye and hand on your possessions and don't wander through obviously rough tough areas of Jakarta. Beware of offers to help find goods or souvenirs you may want unless you don't mind paying a tip and commission. The emergency police number in Jakarta is 110 but if you run into a difficulty it is preferable to contact hotel or travel agency management.

 ## No-no's

Dress discreetly for visiting religious sites and monuments.
Don't act aggressively — remember Indonesian women are modest and not always as 'liberated' as one might think.
Don't breeze into any old Jakarta nightspot.
Don't expect everything to be shiny clean and up to date.

 ## Essentials

Less of a problem to find, more of a problem to pay. As for pure pleasure shopping, Indonesia is one of the best. Its batiks are marvellous. The prints vary from place to place but the best choice is in Jakarta — you can learn about the batik technique by arranging a visit to the Batik Research Institute in Jojakarta. Best city shopping streets are Haji Agus Salim and Jalan Pasar Baru. Bali now produces its own effective beach and resort wear.

 ## Medical Survival

Don't drink the water! Not even with the anti-malaria pills. Outside a hotel, always make sure that any water served (say for tea) is steaming, not luke warm. Eating from food stalls or in hole-in-the-wall restaurants is not recommended if you don't want to risk stomach upsets.

All major hotels retain English-speaking doctors on call and there are good chemists called *Apotiks* in all cities. The ambulance number in Jakarta is 118 but contact hotel management, your holiday rep or the British Embassy first.

 ## What to do Solo

A city sightseeing tour of *Jakarta* will show the old Sunda Kelapa harbour area where Dutch and Portuguese traders first began to compete for a foothold. Their evidence lingers in the gabled houses, the Stadhuis Museum and the 'Portuguese' Church.

There are plenty of markets: fruit and flowers at Cikini Market, antiques on Jalan Surabaya — and small batik factories in the Karet district. 'Dreamland' along the beach is a complex of tourist facilities with its own art market, open air theatre and bowling alley, but 'Indonesia in Miniature' is more likely to interest visitors unable to explore the rest of the country. In replicas of houses from all the provinces you can get an overall view of the country's arts and architecture.

At Jakarta's cultural centre, Taman Ismail Murzuki at Cikini Raya, it is worth seeing some of the more traditional forms of entertainment like the dance dramas (*wayang orang*) and the shadow puppet plays (*wayang kulit*).

Since *Bali* can be reached directly by international flight it is often the prime tourist destination. Its rural areas are still idyllic despite a massive influx of foreigners — a scenic combination of volcanic mountains, rich green forests and rice paddies. Everywhere there are temples — large impressive ornately carved ones, tiny village ones piled high with offerings. By safely bargaining at your hotel for car and driver for the day, you will be able to get away from the more commercialised areas and enjoy the local way of life.

Organised excursions will certainly show some of the major temples. Pura Besakih on the slopes of Mount Agung is the most sacred, reached via a stretch of black sand beaches; other important ones to see include Pura Goa Lawah, Pura Ulu Watu, Pura Batur, Pura Pusering Jagat and Pura Batukaru.

The seasoned traveller will prefer to catch a traditional dance performance during one of the festivals in the temples, but organised presentations are frequently laid on by the major hotels. The most popular dance is the *legong* where girls in bejewelled costumes portray by movement a legendary story of a cruel king and an unwilling princess. The *kecak* or money dance by way of contrast, is performed only by men and look out for the *barong* dance.

The Balinese are renowned for their woodcarvings — some of the best of their work may be seen in the village of Mas.

Most tourist facilities are around Sanur Beach though Nusa Dua has more recently been developed on the southern peninsula. For surfing, Kuta Beach is the best.

Visas and Inoculations

Visas — required.

Inoculations — none compulsory, but typhoid, polio, cholera and malaria pills recommended.

Useful Addresses

Embassies
British Embassy, Jalan Mhthamrin 75, Jakarta 10310. Tel: 330 904
US Embassy, Medea Merdeka Selatan 5, Jakarta. Tel: 360 360

Tourist Offices
Indonesian Tourist Information Centre, 70 New Bond Street, London W1. Tel: 01-629 0862

29 AUSTRALIA AND NEW ZEALAND

Australia is both a continent and an island, a vast country fringed by a population whose manners and attitude would make many a Briton shudder — many a Briton that is who doesn't realise that Australia is not quite as backward as its Outback would suggest. Indeed, Londoners think most of Australia is living in their city, what with the ads and the accents round Earls Court. Australians travel for months at a time — let's face it, home is the other side of the world — and if they don't travel grandly, they cover a grand scale of territory.

Australia has been a harsh country to cultivate, live in and, until our own lifetime, a difficult destination to reach. Today, its cities are cosmopolitan and its restaurants smart. It is a country for outdoor fans and sun lovers, a country for the hardy but one which has given many immigrants a new start, a chance to become rich.

Provincial though some of its outlying areas may be, Australian attitudes have gradually changed, especially towards women. Tough as it sometimes is to get around physically, a woman need feel no temerity in going alone here. As a Commonwealth comprising six states and two territories, its links with Britain have a strength with which only Canada can compete.

If sheep are the first things which come to mind when you think about Australia, no one would fault you, but even more sheep are the golden fleece of New Zealand, a sort of version of Great Britain as it was in the 1950s. A little behind the times when it comes to fashions and trends (some people will say, boring), New Zealand has a safety factor bar none and a geographic layout that includes fjords and mountains, hot springs and cool aqua lakes.

The Male Attitude

Who could be blamed for perceiving an Australian male as the ultimate 'he-man'? Much of the country is untamed, unfit for civilisation, sun-baked and only back-breaking efforts have turned any of it otherwise. Its original colonists were not only political offenders and petty thieves, but hardened criminals. Discovery of gold brought in more rough 'diggers', coarse hard-drinking men prepared to fight for body and soul.

Of course, those times have long since passed although old

ingrained attitudes took a long time to disappear and haven't all yet done so. Few xenophobic traces remain today and the white-only policy has been abandoned whilst surviving Aborigines have become full-fledged Australian citizens. But the average Australian is still a chauvinist only just about used to drinking alongside a woman in a bar (until recently a male preserve). And if you are going to drink alongside, then you're not a little flower but one who's used to direct language and back-slapping.

Australians are easy-going, helpful and tolerant with a distinct distaste for formality and a healthy respect for nature and the elements. They are almost all middle class — pockets of poverty are practically non-existent. Their sense of humour is one of fun but don't be surprised if you're teased for being 'a pommy'. That expression is still used, but nowadays usually in an affectionate way.

As for New Zealanders, you may at first mistake the accent for Australian whilst the male attitude is close to that of an Englishman. There is little racial prejudice so encounters with part or full-blood Maoris is quite probable. A reputation for being warm and friendly without the cut-throat veneer of other nations, has given New Zealanders their popularity amongst foreigners.

Where to Stay

Being able to boast of luxury hostelries was never top priority for either Australia or New Zealand until an increase in business and holiday travel demanded it. Today, major cities in both countries (more so in Australia) can offer the very best of first class accommodation with well organised services and run in an efficient way. Moderately-priced hotels and motels are also of a good standard.

Getting Around on Your Own

By necessity, Australia is a motorised nation (domestic air fares are high), with good roads and services between major cities. Car hire is readily available and most highways are designed for high speed travel. But a word of warning — don't head off into the Outback alone and never travel off the well used roads without spare petrol and bottled water. The bush may look innocent enough but can in fact be terribly treacherous if you get lost in it. By all means, explore, but be prudent.

Train service connects all state capitals and many other urban centres and there is an unbroken link from Sydney to Perth across country. Main line trains have sleeping and dining cars and are air conditioned.

Moving around Sydney may be done by bus, electric train or ferry. Taxis are plentiful for hailing, hiring from an official rank, or booking by phone.

Similarly, New Zealand's main cities are linked by road and rail as well as air. Road travel is exciting and never monotonous and in some places provides the only access (air apart) to the more mountainous regions. Distances are not actually that great but allow plenty of time to cover them — there are few straight stretches and the speed limit is 50 miles per hour. Local hazards include flocks of sheep with right of the road.

Rail service is available in both the North and South Islands. One of the best scenic routes is between Auckland and Wellington (North Island) on the air conditioned Silver Fern which offers hostess-service.

Eating and Drinking Solo

Since the Second World War, Australian eating and drinking habits, in its restaurants and water holes, have changed for the better. Gone is the old grill serving meat and vegetables and in its place a wide choice of restaurants serving ethnic cuisine, cafés and bistros, and wine bars, in any of which no woman will be looked at askance.

Melbourne's restaurants especially are award winners, though many require you bring your own wine or booze. Wherever you go, the seafood is freshly excellent — evidenced by Sydney oysters to name but one choice and, naturally enough, lamb is world famous. Try a 'floater', the closest to a national dish — a rather greasy but delicious meat pie doused with ketchup.

With the changing times and influx of immigrants has come the delicatessens, as good as you'll find anywhere. Also the development of wine, now a favourite tipple of Australians themselves. An increased liking for wine in New Zealand has improved the taste of the local plonk as well.

The Safety Factor

Your personal safety should not be a worry. Whilst crime is not unheard of on the other side of the world, the rate is low and policemen do not carry guns. Of far greater concern are physical safety precautions — being wary of the Outback; not swimming either when it is not recommended by flag, or in currents that are only suited to the expert; watching out for jellyfish.

No-no's

Don't stay unprotected too long in the sunshine.
Don't head off into the bush (or New Zealand's mountains) by yourself.
Watch out for the redback spider in Australia.
Don't gape at an Aborigine.
Don't carelessly toss away a cigarette — it could cause a bush fire.

 ## Essentials

No essential item is difficult to find or replace in either country — you'll find plenty of imported cosmetics and toiletries in every department store. Only in the isolated places will you need to be completely prepared. Service laundry is quite expensive but motels usually have coin-operated machines. There's no lack of hairdressers in any of the major cities.

Don't forget the seasons are reversed 'Down Under' so that temperature changes can be extreme. Sydney weather is not very predictable but Wellington in New Zealand is always windy.

Electricity: 220-250v, 50 cycles.

 ## Medical Survival

The standards of medical care in both countries is exceedingly high. Top hotels have a doctor on call for emergencies or you could go to the the casualty department of a local hospital. Australia's Royal Flying Doctor Service provides medical attention to those living in outlying areas. A plus factor in New Zealand (where medical services and most prescribed medicines are free) is that visitors who are injured in an accident will be compensated regardless of whose fault the accident was.

 ## What to do Solo

Sydney is undoubtedly the most cosmopolitan of Australia's cities, and one of the most beautiful, reminiscent as it is of San Francisco. One of the most pleasant trips is by boat around the famous harbour on a coffee cruise. Another way is to take the 'Sydney Explorer' around the city's main tourist spots — you can get on and off at will with the same-day ticket. For an overall view, ascend Sydney Tower which has two observation levels and two revolving restaurants.

One of the most interesting, easy-to-walk-around districts is The Rocks where the city began. It has been renovated and redeveloped into an area of art galleries, shops and inexpensive restaurants. The oldest building, Cadman's Cottage, is located here and in the Argyle Centre, craftsmen exhibit and sell their work.

Many Sydney names are British ones — hence Hyde Park, an open space in the inner city and King's Cross, the nightlife centre, or Paddington, a delightful village-like residential district. Women are advised not to visit King's Cross at night without an escort as it can be rough and sleazy.

Local buses to smart suburbs like Point Pyper and Double Bay are easy and cheap to use. The most famous ocean beach is Bondi, of course, but it is only one of many south of the harbour. There are also beaches to the north such as Manley but these are slightly further away.

Australia's two most other important cities for the tourist are *Melbourne* and *Perth*. Package tours often take in Alice Springs in the middle of the country for a look at *Ayers Rock,* or Cairns — the base for exploring the *Great Barrier Reef.* No one should miss a visit to at least one sheep station where shearing and boomerang demonstrations are given, nor a tour of some of Australia's vineyards where several vintners welcome visitors and offer tastings.

New Zealand's largest city, *Auckland,* is situated on a slim isthmus separating two seas — the Pacific and the Tasman. Its main street is Queen Street and its main attraction is Mount Eden, an extinct volcano from whose summit there is a circular panoramic view. Harbour cruises leave from the Ferry Building for parts of the Hauraki Gulf.

In the North Island, your main objective should be the *Bay of Islands* to the north of Aukland where Paihia has become a holiday centre. Regular launch service connects it with Russell and from either base, launch and catamaran cruises operate to outlying islands. Both types of boat have comfortable cabins, bars and hostess service.

To the south of Aukland, *Rotorua* is of prime worth for its thermal springs. The smell of sulphur is a little overpowering but harmless. The main area of geysers and spouting boiling mud is in Whakarewarewa whose Pohutu Geyser is New Zealand's largest, shooting up to 100 ft. Rotorua is also a traditional Maori homeland so you can expect to find Maori crafts for sale and evening dance performances.

At the heart of the country and the biggest attraction in South Island is *Mount Cook,* first climbed by a woman in 1913. One of the best ways to see it is by ski plane which lands on vast snowfields at the head of a glacier. Another scenic flight takes you over Milford Sound near picturesque Queenstown. If fear of flying proves too much, take one of the launch cruises instead.

Visas and Inoculations

Visas — required for Australia; none required for New Zealand.
Inoculations — none required.

Useful Addresses

Embassies
British High Commission, Commonwealth Avenue, Canberra, ACT 2600, Australia. Tel: 73 04 22
British High Commission, 2 The Terrace, PO Box 1812, Wellington, New Zealand. Tel: 726 049
US Embassy, Moonah Place, Canberra ACT 2600, Australia. Tel: 705 000
US Embassy, 29 Fitzherbert Terrace, Thorndon, Wellington, New Zealand. Tel: 722 068

Tourist Offices
Australian National Tourist Office, 30 St George Street, London W1. Tel: 01-629 0461
Australian Tourist Commission, 630 Fifth Avenue, New York, NY 10017. Tel: (212) 489 7550
New Zealand High Commission, New Zealand House, Haymarket, London SW1. Tel: 01-930 8422

THE AMERICAS

The style and gamut of the Americas runs from the sublime to the ridiculous so far as the female traveller is concerned. The North American continent always seems bigger and bolder than Europe and is almost certainly more technologically advanced. Its familiarity lends an advantage despite city tensions.

South America, on the other hand, is changeable, capricious in its rules and atmosphere, and its politics. Much of it is near virgin territory, reason enough to add a dash of excitement to travels within any of its countries.

The exotic compromise is Mexico where Mayan tales weave an irresistible spell and yet another compromise, the islands of the Caribbean. The pleasures of investigating the Americas far outweigh the dangers.

30 CANADA

It is surprising that even the most intelligent people forget how large Canada is. In fact, it is the world's second largest country still laying claim to vast stretches of pure wilderness and isolated fishing communities. In Canada there are two official languages and several dominant cultures — an outdoor playground that would need plenty of time for proper exploration.

Being part of the North American continent, it is easy enough to reach and is used to independent travellers. In many ways it seems designed for those on their own — in the desolate areas, many are. For you, of course, this could just mean lonely so select a province carefully before jetting off. The Northwest Territories and Yukon, for example, are scarcely visited by tourists since these are the wilds of interest to hunters and fishermen. British Columbia and Alberta, on the other hand, are a favourite scenic destination, offering the Rockies, farms and ranches and that jewel of a vacation city, Vancouver. The maritime provinces with their seafaring traditions are the summer mecca but the most popular provinces are Ontario and Quebec.

Quebec is French Canada ... French speaking, French cooking, French volatile. Ontario is British-influenced but its key city, Toronto, has blossomed in recent decades into a lively city for the arts.

The Male Attitude

The average Canadian is a curious mixture of English and American temperaments. Sporty and fairly conservative, he has the same materialistic streak as the neighbours with a love for gadgets and convenient living, a respect for efficiency and things that work. Canadians for some reason appear to lack the glamour and dazzle of Americans (and their country reflects it), but they are just as kind and helpful, friendly and even more clean living. He is less 'loud' and brash, keeps stronger ties with Britain and tends to maintain deeper relationships. The general view that Canadians are harmless but not humourless is probably correct.

The French Canadian is inclined to be more volatile and emotional, more likely to wave his arms around and rap a table to stress a point. More fun loving and sometimes more bad tempered, he is nevertheless not so disdainful as his true French counterpart and does not share his style.

Where to Stay

Standards of accommodation in Canada are excellent with a wide choice of hotels in all styles and price brackets in the major cities. Chain names like Hilton, Sheraton, Holiday Inn are evident everywhere, some being particularly geared to convention business such as the Sheraton Centre and Hilton Harbour Castle, both in Toronto. Canada's own top companies are Four Season, CN Hotels and CP Hotels. A number of the latter are old landmark hotels simulating Châteaux such as Château Lake Louise on the west coast and Château Frontenac in Quebec City.

Rates at city hotels are usually on a room-only basis but resort and country areas may offer half or full board. A number of resort properties are located in Ontario but don't be misled by the word 'inn'. A Canadian inn is much larger than those we're used to in the UK and can be quite plush.

Smaller inns or guest houses are a feature in the Maritimes where farms also take in paying guests. Farm and ranch accommodation is also prevalent in British Columbia and Alberta. Self-catering accommodation in Canada is known as 'housekeeping cottages', often around the lake regions but by reason of their very nature, can be lonesome. Those seeking tranquillity or the adventure of the wilds can find friendly fishing lodges and fly-in camps in the north, and camp sites in spectacular settings. In western parks, there are luxury lodges with recreational facilities and planned activities on their own grounds. All highways are well serviced with motels.

Getting Around on Your Own

Canada's transport system is organised enough not to give headaches. Internal flights are provided by national airlines and regional carriers on a scheduled and charter basis, connecting major cities and even far-flung points.

Car hire is readily available and recommendable for getting around since most roads are very good. The speed limit for controlled access highways varies from 90 to 100 km per hour; 80 km for other highways and in urban areas between 40 and 60 km. Your only warning is bad weather conditions. Camper or motorhome hire is perfectly feasible, too, and manageable if you rent the smaller type of vehicle.

Extensive rail service operates right across Canada, often the preferred way of seeing the country since many of the routes (especially out west) are scenic and observation cars allow you to take advantage of the views. Such long-distance trains are comfortable, safe and feature dining cars, sleeping cars and large picture windows. Inter-city service is equally good.

Cost-effective coach travel covers routes in all parts of the country including coast-to-coast, and is frequently used for holiday packages with and without escort guides.

In some places, boating may be the most favourable method of travel for Canada's waterways are legion. I have only to mention the Inside Passage, St Lawrence Seaway and the Trent-Severn Waterway to name but some.

Eating and Drinking Solo

Certainly no problem finding a place to suit your mood or budget. Restaurants range from fast food to high society. Montreal, Toronto and Vancouver all have a selection of bistros and brasseries, courtyard and pavement cafés where you'll feel perfectly at home. Recommended areas include the Yorkville section of Toronto, the old quarter of Montreal and the waterfront area of Vancouver, or the old part of Quebec City. In the Maritimes you may be best off joining a community lobster supper. So-called singles bars are also a feature of major cities.

Most cities have ethnic quarters and markets and all follow the American way by designating watering holes as cocktail lounges, rather than as bars. The food itself comes in American-sized portions and includes plenty of fish and first class beef. Canadian staples include a buckwheat cake breakfast with home-produced ham and maple syrup, but out in the sticks of Newfoundland, menu oddities include moose meat soup and cod tongues!

Canadian beer is slightly stronger than American — Molson's and Lablatt are two popular labels. In recent years domestic wine has improved to the point of being palatable — most of it comes from the Niagara Peninsula.

The Safety Factor

As a whole, Canada is a safe country to travel in. It isn't, of course, totally crime-free but where is? Reassuringly, its cities have a low crime rate and a reputation for cleanliness and safety. The police number varies from region to region but is generally posted on telephones including public ones, or simply dial 0 and ask for the police.

No-no's

Don't bother to bring your coat if shopping underground in Montreal or Toronto — the complexes are inter-linked and warm no matter how harsh the weather outside.

Don't automatically assume you can change sterling at a hotel — you may need a bank.

Don't expect swimming waters to be very warm even at the height of summer.

 ## Essentials

Anything you want, you'll find — everywhere except the most desolate areas. Canada's shopping malls are among the world's finest and stock many British and French goods besides their own. In Montreal, the three major underground complexes are Place Ville-Marie, Place Bonaventure and Complexe Desjardins. In Toronto, in addition to Eaton Centre, The Lanes and the TD Centre are worth looking into. Laundry and other services, beauty salons, etc. are bountiful.

Electricity: 110v, 60 cycles

 ## Medical Survival

No sweat finding a doctor — just paying him. The best hotels will call for one, or look in the Yellow Pages, but make sure you're fully insured for health. Chemists are plentiful (sometimes known as pharmacies) and at least one will stay open late in major tourist centres, but closing times vary from region to region. There may be some difficulty in rural areas. Water is safe to drink throughout Canada.

 ## What to do Solo

Overlook *Toronto* from its gleaming landmark, the CN Tower, which houses an observation level, revolving restaurant and discothèque plus an excellent simulated space flight attraction at its base. At Harbourfront, there's plenty to do from browsing through the outdoor summer antique market to sipping a drink overlooking Lake Ontario or looking at one of the exhibitions that take place here. Further along the lakefront, Ontario Place screens a variety of presentations in its Cinesphere Theatre and holds concerts under the stars in summer.

Since Toronto is laid out in a grid system, you can't really get lost. Simply remember that the two main streets are Yonge and Bloor, both good for shops and entertainment. If the weather's good, walk around Yorkville's boutiques and galleries, wander through the city's tiny Chinatown and drop in at the St Lawrence Market.

Toronto can offer a host of museums including the celebrated Science Museum and the Art Gallery of Ontario. As an arts centre it's tops in Canada with an opera season at O'Keefe Centre from September to June and concerts given in Roy Thomson Hall.

You can relive childhood out of town at Canada's Wonderland, a theme park with thrill rides and live entertainment, or take a trip to Black Creek Pioneer Village, just one of Canada's recreated examples of life as it used to be. During the summer re-enacted military life, complete with battle drills, cannon firings and parades, takes place at Old Fort York.

In *Montreal,* the liveliest streets are Crescent, Prince-Arthur, Duluth and Saint-Denis. Best place to walk around is Old Montreal whose warehouses have been converted into jazz bars and boutiques. The city's landmark is Mount Royal Park where carriages wait to take you on tour and whose terrace near Lake Beaver is the stage for summer folk dance shows.

Other major city centres are Quebec and Vancouver. The country's best beaches are on Prince Edward Island; its best ski areas around Banff and Lake Louise. Most astounding annual event is the Calgary Stampede, but don't expect to find a room at the last moment. Canada is a very sporting country with masses of fishing and canoeing opportunities, forests, national parks and winter holiday pursuits. Sport apart, remember October is the end of season when many of the country's outdoor attractions close.

Visas and Inoculations

Visas — none required.
Inoculations — none required.

Useful Addresses

Embassies
British Embassy, 80 Elgin Street, Ottawa K1P 5K7. Tel: 237 1530
US Embassy, 100 Wellington Street, Ottawa. Tel: 238 6335

Tourist Offices
Canadian High Commission, Canada House, Trafalgar Square, London SW1. Tel: 01-629 9492
Canadian Government Travel Bureau, 1251 Avenue of the Americas, New York, NY 10020. Tel: (212) 757 3583

31 USA

Of all the countries in the world, America has to be the easiest and most friendly for the independent visitor. No, its cities aren't the safest but its language and its outlook are more comprehensible and its food and products oh so familiar.

Just as we can fault Americans' judgement of distance in the UK, so vice versa is true. Don't expect to take in New York and Florida and San Francisco and Hawaii — unless you have a lot of time or make a whirlwind tour. Remember it takes almost as long by air to cross from one coast to another as it does to travel to the USA from the UK.

Nor does New York City sum up all of America, a vast and varied country with as many personality contrasts as it has physical ones. Despite what it might think of itself, by European standards America is very young, a teenager grown tall and healthy in an incredibly short time, but still a teenager. A melting pot result of intermingling nationalities still in search of an identity.

The Male Attitude

One can usually tell the average American abroad by what he wears. A bright plaid jacket and white shoes (whatever the month and the weather) are good signals. A visor-ed cap and Hawaiian-style shirt will signify he's on holiday; a video camera will record every merry moment.

The American comes on strong. He'll first tell you all about his life, then ask about yours. He can be direct enough to ask you to bed after just a short while of knowing you and call you frigid when you decline. Yet at heart he tends to be insecure and prudish.

As an escort, he may not be as attentive as you'd like; as a host, he couldn't be more hospitable. Americans establish relationships quickly, but don't always keep them up — out of sight is very often out of mind and today's curiosity and interest can be just a flash in the pan.

But Americans are a helpful nation, going out of their way to help a damsel in distress, offering a night's shelter or food without a moment's hesitation. And the male stranger who instigates a conversation may just want to talk, and could wind up your closest confidante. If Americans are considered loud and brash, it's because they know far less formality than Europeans, but don't think a class system doesn't exist within their own ranks. Not mere money either, but family name and birthplace not to mention school and college background ... witness all the nickname tags we've borrowed: Yaps and Yuppies, preppies, Ivy League.

You'll encounter regional differences too. The Texans, full of thick-skinned ego; New Yorkers, brittle to the apple's core; Californians, laid back and fancy free; southerners permeating softer manners with the southern drawl; midwesterners, down to salty earth. In America, you will encounter bible-belt fanatics, aggressive salesmen and amoral adventurers — in other words, a many-threaded tapestry of people.

Where to Stay

If biggest is best, America can boast it. Gigantic hotels with hundreds of rooms, designed for conventioneers and operating so slickly other countries could learn a thing or two. American luxury chain hotels have done wonders world-wide with their management know-how and their creature comforts. Hilton, Sheraton, Intercontinental, Marriott and Hyatt — are all American names operating highly respected much favoured properties across the globe. Business-minded glossy American hotels were the first to feature business centres and executive floors. They have always been the first to offer the most advanced technological achievements, the most fashionable designs — greenery-filled atriums and panoramic exterior elevators, computerised reservation systems and mini bars. Every major American city can offer a broad range of top bracket hotels.

What makes a hotel top notch, however, perhaps varies from the European idea. It may well be size or number of chandeliers to decorate the lobby or amount of marble. The glitzier it is the better it is and only recently has a Europeanised 'style' crept in to somewhere like New York where suddenly the Meridien and Elysee are chic. Only recently have the older hotels recognised they are a novelty and invested money to restore former grandeur.

Since Americans demand comfort, even the middle range of hotels offer unsurpassed quality and value for money. Many of these belong to chains and are motels, putting our own British ones to shame. Quality Inns, Days Inns, Howard Johnsons, Ramada are all to be reckoned with. Motels that don't even bear a familiar sign are rewarding with their double doubles or water beds, their coffee shops and swimming pools.

Self-catering is not much in evidence but bed and breakfast is on the increase. Few inns can offer years of history or four-poster beds but they can provide a homely atmosphere and family dinners at a favourably comparable price to their newer neighbours.

A particular type of American accommodation is 'the resort', a place to stay that can offer all kinds of entertainment and recreational facilities on its own premises ... innumerable in Florida and Hawaii. And then there are the ranches — working ones, dude ones, family guest ones for whom the key is riding the trail western style, learning lasso tricks and watching a rodeo ... innumerable in Texas and Arizona.

Getting Around on Your Own

The car is king in America and the network of roads and superhighways couldn't be better, couldn't be more serviced. In addition to the internationally known car hire companies, each state has local ones whose prices may be better. (Since states make some of their own laws, minimum driving age may vary from 21 to 25.) Some companies allow car pickup in one state, drop-off in another; some are rated for unlimited mileage, some by the mile.

Superhighways may be called Interstates, Turnpikes or Expressways but as much as the broad multi-laned roads might tempt you to speed, remember that the maximum speed limit is 55 miles per hour, that police patrol is strict and fines, fierce. Most rental cars are automatic and often larger than those the British are used to which may cause a few initial problems. Driving is to the right. The fly/drive packages offered by British tour operators are among the most economical ways of seeing the USA.

Flying from place to place will save time and can save money even when you have not pre-purchased an air pass abroad. Domestic airlines constantly offer special fares for specific flights like 'red eye specials'. Check with a travel agent before buying.

Taking the train is not the cheapest method of getting around but it is one of the most scenic and comfortable. Amtrak's network (honed down as it is), spreads throughout the country and on long-distance routes superliners offer sleepers with private toilet and shower, observation cars, bar and dining cars. There are such trains with magical names: the Broadway Limited from New York to Chicago; the Silver Meteor from New York to Miami; the Crescent from New York to Atlanta and New Orleans; or the San Francisco Zephyr. The high-speed Metroliner is the most recommendable way to reach Washington, DC from New York.

Travelling America by coach is the cheapest, most extensive way and one by which you will certainly meet a host of very different people. Greyhound and Trailways are the two biggest names in coaching, operating not only from point to point, city to city, but also featuring package tours. A woman prepared for a gamut of seat companions and able to cope with what is often a seedy bus terminus, will find coach travel safe enough, but other tourists apart, is unlikely to come across too many middle class, professional-background passengers.

Public transportation in cities varies, but there's always a local bus service, sometimes an express bus service to and from suburban areas; trams are kept more for touristic purposes than any other, as in San Francisco; and subway (ill advised for night time travel in New York).

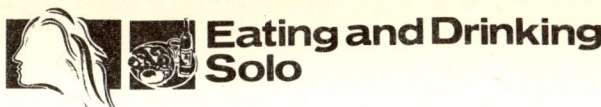

Eating and Drinking Solo

America is *the* land for fast food and everyone but everyone, from young singles to family parties, uses McDonald's, Arbee's, Kentucky Fried Chicken, Aunt Jemima's Pancakes — or any of the other outlets located along the motorways and in the towns and cities. Eating in almost any of them is practically inescapable and perhaps the most suitable alternative to a lonely room service supper.

Countless people on their own eat at diners and coffee shops, both of which offer counter service as well as table. Thanks to an American obsession with hygiene, you can safely choose the sleaziest looking truck-stop diner and be sure of wholesome food at a reasonable price. Coffee shops, chain or otherwise, are usually licensed to sell liquor as well as soft beverages with food that ranges from overstuffed sandwiches to daily specials. Steak and ale house chains with all-you-can-eat salad bars are another option.

Wherever you eat you won't suffer from bad service because you're a woman alone. The cities' better restaurants actually go out of their way to put you at your ease and ensure you have everything you need. Cafés, pubs and singles bars thrive on your patronage. Dark and panelled, airy and glassed in or spilling onto sidewalks, they can almost all be recommended. In a cocktail lounge (far more prevalent than a straightforward bar) you need only be bothered as much as you allow for bar tenders and managers keep a protective, sometimes fatherly eye on female guests.

The drinking age varies from state to state with a minimum of 18. A few areas of the USA have remained 'dry' with no liquor available and in some establishments, only beer or wine is sold or you may have to bring in your own.

The Safety Factor

What can one say about a country which grew and flourished on violence, is notable for drug problems and freakish behaviour, whose police carry firearms, whose gangsters made history? All one can say is take reasonable care and guidance as to where you walk alone and what hours you travel. Lock and chain all hotel doors — don't open to anyone you don't know or aren't expecting. Stay away from obviously dangerous areas such as docklands, seedy and run down areas, parks at night, or neighbourhoods that are quiet and dark. Carry some cash (but not too much) — Americans call it 'mugging money' and be on the lookout for light fingered pickpockets at street markets. In an emergency dial 0 and ask for whichever service you need, or 911 for the police.

 ## No-no's

If your car stalls at night, remain inside with the door locked — don't get out — and when help does stop, make sure the samaritan is really a good one.
Don't travel the New York subway alone at night.
Don't walk through New York's Central Park at night, nor its more isolated areas during the day.
Don't try to bribe police when stopped for an offence.
Don't do anything reckless — an accident can cost a lot.
Don't wear jodhpurs for a ranching holiday — they'll laugh.

 ## Essentials

Any article that can be bought can be bought in America — no one lacks for anything here. One-day cleaning services and while-you-wait pressing services are available outside of hotels as well as in. Coin-operated launderettes and beauty salons are ubiquitous.
Electricity: 110-115v, 60 cycles.

 ## Medical Survival

Medical care in the USA is of a very high standard but a very high price. Make sure you're fully insured. Finding a doctor is not a problem, either through your hotel or the yellow pages, or by dialling the operator. Most towns have at least one drugstore which is open late, sometimes 24 hours, and on a Sunday.

 ## What to do Solo

In *New York*, take a do-it-yourself walking tour of Lower Manhattan during daylight hours — it's New York's most historic area and a suggested routing is provided free by the New York Visitors and Convention Bureau. Along the way, drop in to South Street Seaport, a renovated area with a Covent Garden-style market, restaurants and an open air sailing museum. Or join an organised, escorted walking tour of Harlem — the most recommended way to see the sights of Upper Manhattan.

Spend the day in Greenwich Village's coffee houses and boutiques or browse the art galleries in SoHo. Buy a tour of Rockefeller Center and see the multi-media screen presentation, 'The New York Experience'. Spend the evening at Radio City Music Hall (famous for its high-kicking Rockettes), but take a taxi home. Listen to a concert, attend opera or ballet at Lincoln Center or see a theatre matinée performance for maybe half price if you queue early enough at Times Square for same-day performance.

Manhattan offers innumerable museums to suit all tastes — some like the Met you could literally spend hours in. Equally, numerous tours will show you city sights or back-stage happenings. A popular way of enjoying a day alone is to sail around Manhattan on a Circle Line cruise, or on a harbour cruise from South Street Seaport.

Shop in the city's famous complexes like the Trump Tower and explore the world's largest department store, Macy's. Many stores are open Sundays and frequently hold sales. Beware, though, of small shop announcements that they're closing down — discounts are rarely genuine.

Take a cable car in *San Francisco* to Fisherman's Wharf where you can buy a tub of fresh seafood and watch the human circus that is always going on here. Visit Mission Dolores, take a ferry to Alcatraz or drive north to the wine country of Napa Valley. From Union Square it's an easy stroll to Chinatown (America's largest Oriental community) or see it all from a helicopter.

In *New Orleans* your own feet are the best way to get around the French Quarter, though you could take a carriage ride from Jackson Square. This lively city keeps up a frantic pace all night long so walking along Royal and Bourbon Streets poses no great danger. Drop in and listen to jazz at Preservation Hall, buy a take-away drink from any bar, and don't miss brunch at Antoine's. Coffee and beignets are a must at the French Market by the side of the Mississippi where you can watch barges move on up river.

America has something for everyone from mountains (the Sierras, the Smokies) to deserts (Death Valley) to beautiful beaches (Florida's Pinellas and Miami coast). There are natural wonders like the Grand Canyon and man-made ones like Disneyland and Disney World. Theme parks present thrill rides or perhaps living history; national parks contain some of the finest camping facilities, surrounded by unbeatable scenery.

Visas and Inoculations

Visas — required.
Inoculations — none required.

Useful Addresses

Embassies
UK Consulate, 845 Third Avenue, New York, NY 10022, Tel: (212) 752 5747

Tourist Offices
United States Travel & Tourism, 22 Sackville Street, London W1. Tel: 01-439 7433
United States of America Embassy, 24 Grosvenor Square, London W1. Immigrant and Visitor Visa Enquiries: 01-499 3443

32 MEXICO

Mexico has always proved it's a survivor — even its most recent earthquakes have not diminished its power of appeal. It is a diverse country which has seen countless single women, from hippies to the more studious interested in its ancient culture, breeze through its cities and resorts.

It is not the easiest country to get to know, learn to love or tour on one's own. Too much corruption, too much poverty and too much indolence can place obstacles in the path of the traveller bent on seeing a variety of destinations in any other way than by an escorted tour.

Having said that, Mexico is well used to tourists (particularly from the USA) and is very commercialised in centres like Acapulco, Puerto Vallarta or Guadalajara. Such centres boast excellent facilities and efficiently planned and executed excursions.

The Male Attitude

It is as well to know that this is a major Spanish-speaking country and knowledge of that language will stand you in good stead. The ethnic mix includes Indian and black blood besides white European, so the average Mexican's attitude incorporates a little of everything. The dominant religion, however, is Roman Catholic — an average attitude is, therefore, based on all the major characteristics of that faith: i.e. a sense of moral duty, love of family, etc.

By way of mixed blood possibly, the Mexican male is volatile, in turns aggressive and sensitive, lazy yet sometimes razor-edge sharp when it comes to business acumen. A power complex often leads to taking what he wants, whether it be somebody else's property or a woman. Be warned! Self-indulgence has led to millionaires' row — and to bankruptcy.

Where to Stay

There are exceptionally fine luxury hotels in all the major centres — Mexico City's most expensive are found in the Zona Rosa and along Avenida Insurgentes Sur. In all the service is good and facilities are geared to both business and holiday markets. The capital also has a few motels. Like Mexico City, the most popular resort, Acapulco is full of skyscrapers and de luxe hotels which fill to the seams in January and February. English is spoken in all the best hotels.

There are many small hotels or pensions available at bargain rates in less busy centres, but it is best to obtain a recommended list of accommodation from the tourist office.

Getting Around on Your Own

The best train service is the Pullman between Mexico City and Monterrey, Gaudalajara, Veracruz and Mérida; the rest is pretty slow. Book first class if you want any kind of air conditioning and reclining seats and look for trains with sleeper cars or *alcobas* (better berths). Second class travel is not recommended if only for the thievery rife on Mexican trains.

Although there are three types of bus, a first class one is suggested (book well in advance and be prepared for lengthy queueing time for the ticket). First class buses usually have a toilet on board and supposedly are air conditioned (it often doesn't work). Second class buses often break down and should only be used by those seeking an 'interesting' experience.

Car hire is readily available but recommended only for use on major highways. Taxis are cheap, but even when metered do not use them. Taking taxis is a little like Russian roulette since many drivers do not speak English and may not know the address you give. Always arrange the price in advance, including those 'Tourismo' taxis which line up outside major hotels. Shared taxis (*peseros*) often operate (as in Mexico City) on specific routes. Flag them down — they'll stop if they have an empty seat.

Mexico City has its own local bus, tram and metro system.

Eating and Drinking Solo

Mexico is the easiest place to get a tummy upset without thinking about it, so be careful where you eat outside of hotels. Chinese restaurants are likely to be the cleanest. The country's cuisine, though, can be interesting and elaborate — not just *tamales*, *tacos*, *enchiladas* and *tortillas*. Lunch is the heaviest and longest meal of the day — budgeteers should ask for the *comida corrida* (daily specials).

Except for tourist spots, there are few outdoor cafés or drinking spots. The cheapest beverages include Mexican beer whose best brands are Bavaria, Bohemia, XXX, Superior and Tecate. The national drink, *tequila* is also reasonable but is an acquired taste, and I suggest you pass up the powerful *pulque* and *mescal*.

The Safety Factor

Apart from normal city precautions, theft is the biggest worry. In Mexico you really do have to keep an eagle eye on possessions: in your hotel room, on the buses and trains, in the streets. Anything and everything can disappear in a flash.

Mexicans are very inclined to the 'backhander'. If you are stopped by the police for an offence you didn't commit (this often happens to drivers), refuse to pay the on the spot 'fine' and insist on going to the tourist police headquarters.

No-no's

Don't hitchhike alone.
Don't let a stranger help find you a hotel — the room rate will go up.
Don't use the Mexico City metro alone.
Don't take photos in the metro — you could be arrested.

Essentials

No problem at all in finding any item you may need. In Mexico City the most fashionable shops are in the Zona Rosa bounded by Paseo de la Reforma, Av. Chapultepec, Calle Florencia and Calle Nápoles. There are also good shops on 5 de Mayo, 16 de Septiembre, Insurgentes and Colonia Juárez. Best buys are on quality suede and leather or perfume.

Electricity is 125v, 60 cycles in Mexico City; mostly 110-120v elsewhere.

Medical Survival

Beware of the altitude and don't overdo the eating and drinking in any high place like the capital. Very definitely don't drink the water — mineral water is sold throughout the country, bottled — plain or flavoured — Tehuacán is a first class brand. Avoid raw vegetables and don't eat any fruit you can't peel. (Foodstuffs sold on the streets are temptingly cheap but dangerous to the system). Milk also is only safe when it comes in sealed containers marked *pasteurizado*.

The best hotels will recommend an English-speaking doctor, or in Mexico City you can go to the Clinica Prensa for a consultation or medicine. The Farmacia Homeopática on Calle Mesones is open 24 hours.

What to do Solo

At the centre of *Mexico City* is the Zocalo or main square where many celebrations are held — always full of people. All city sightseeing trips stop here to look at the Palacio Nacional, a vast colonial-baroque building famous for its Diego Rivera murals. Best place for a view of the city and Alameda Gardens is the bar at the top of Torre Latino-americana, across the road from Palacio de Bellas Artes. The latter is the place to see the celebrated Mexican Folklore Ballet.

You may well wish to spend a lot of your own time in Chapultepec Park (at the end of Paseo de la Reforma) which contains an amusement park, botanical garden and several museums. The castle that tops the hill in the park is these days the National Museum of History and half-way down the hill is the Gallery of Mexican History. It is, however, the Anthropological Museum which is really splendid.

Mexico City wouldn't be Mexico City without its markets — every district has one but the largest of all is the Mercado Merced, dating back 400 years and whose activities take up several blocks.

Of the many landmarks and monuments to be seen in the city, the most venerated shrine is the Basilica of Guadalupe where it is said the Virgin appeared to the Indian Juan Diego in 1531, imprinting her form (in the guise of an Indian princess) on his cloak — now set in gold at the centre of the magnificent altar.

A worthwhile excursion from the city takes you to the Teotihuacán Pyramids. Here the Pyramid of the Sun covers the same amount of ground as Egypt's Cheops! Son et Lumière performances are given here.

Shopping for silver is something to do everywhere in Mexico but the famous 'silver town' is *Taxco*, a picturesque gem of a town built around twisting cobbled streets. Go here on an organised tour from Mexico City.

One of the most interesting centres in the Yucután is *Mérida*, founded in 1542 on the site of the Mayan city of Tihoo. Like most Mexican cities, it has a central plaza and several markets. Go early to the Mérida Market for good made-to-measure deerskin sandals and panama hats. Calle 65 is the main shopping street; the Museum of Peninsular Culture (for contemporary crafts) is worth visiting. Concerts are given in the open air theatre in the Park of the Americas and free music may be listened to in Plaza Santa Lucia on Thursday evenings.

The resort where women won't feel lonely is *Acapulco* which stretches for ten or so miles over bays and cliffs. The heat can be overpowering but most of the hotels are situated as high as possible to take advantage of any breeze.

Acapulco is an expensively smart resort around its top hotels with fashionable shops and nightclubs (not to mention a red light district). The two most crowded (and popular) of the resort's 20 odd sandy beaches are Caleta and Los Hornos where all forms of watersports are available. One of the biggest attractions is to watch the boys dive into shallow water from the Quebrada. Pleasant boat trips to take include one to Puerto Marques, bay cruises or a glass-bottom boat trip to La Roqueta Island.

Visas and Inoculations

Visas — none required.
Inoculations — none compulsory, but malaria pills, typhoid and polio recommended.

Useful Addresses

Embassies
British Embassy, Calle Rio Lerma 71, Mexico City. Tel: 511 4880
US Embassy, Paseo de la Reforma 305, Mexico City. Tel: 211 0042

Tourist Offices
Mexico Ministry of Tourism, 7 Cork Street, London W1. Tel: 01-734 1058
Mexico National Tourist Council, 405 Park Avenue, New York, NY 10022. Tel: (212) 755 7212

33 CARIBBEAN

The Caribbean is an 'area' but it comprises myriad islands, almost all of which have become year round holiday destinations. Some are grouped together but each has its own identity, and characteristics. Because of their scenery and sunshine, they are considered terribly romantic and for this reason perhaps best seen with a partner. But the major islands are well developed, have seen tourists for decades, indeed depend upon tourism for their economies so being solo shouldn't preclude a visit.

Do be aware that the self-governing British colony and garden island of Bermuda actually lies in the Atlantic and is not endowed with the same winter warmth as its southern sisters. Nor are the Bahamas, strictly speaking, in the Caribbean — or Puerto Rico. The American and British Virgin Islands are generally to be found in Caribbean listings.

To the south, the Leewards, Windwards and West Indies have been influenced by different nationalities. For instance, the best known Dutch islands are Curaçao, Aruba and Bonaire; the best known French islands are Martinique and Guadeloupe. (St Martin/St Maarten is half French, half Dutch). Of those with British connections, Antigua, Barbados, Jamaica, Grenada, St Lucia, Trinidad and St Vincent stand out, but spare a thought for more newly developed Nevis, Caymans and Anguilla.

The Male Attitude

If the attitude is laid back, put it down to the heat. In most of the islands, time doesn't seem to matter. Things may get done — eventually, but a shrug is the most expressive way of saying 'no can do'. Unfortunately, not all the Caribbean is as happy-go-lucky as either it used to be or we are led to believe. Tourism, as always, brought perils with it and some of the island people have become overly enthusiastic about the almighty dollar, and this has led to crime.

The black Caribbean male can be a nuisance, if you're alone on the beach or in a nightclub. Flattered into believing his own prowess by white females (often Canadian) who descend upon the islands literally to get laid, he frequently assumes that every woman has the same thing on her mind. So be warned and be firm.

# Where to Stay

Caribbean hotels are not quite as elitist (or should I say, snobbish) as they were in the days when only a wealthy handful could afford to stay at them. But they can be glamorous, witness Antigua's St James Club, Jamaica's Couples, St Lucia's La Toc, or any of those properties along Barbados' Platinum Coast.

Except for the very small islands with little choice of accommodation, most hotels these days are rated on a room only or at the very most, half board plan. But you will find self-catering complexes and small guest houses — particularly good in Antigua, St Lucia and Barbados with exceptionally fine villas in Jamaica. You will also find Club Meds in Martinique and Guadeloupe (both départements of France) which could well be the Caribbean answer for single women.

Speed and good service are not exactly Caribbean fortes so don't expect staff to come running at a finger snap. In islands where facilities and infrastructure are poor, the plumbing does break down, telephones don't work, lights may go out and water shortages can cause inconvenience. In the very small islands, this all might be considered part of the charm — the kind of Robinson Crusoeish existence that was here before the jets arrived.

# Getting Around on Your Own

In many cases, you won't need to get around too much, since shops and beach are generally within walking distance from your resort hotel and, in the case of organised excursions, you'll be picked up at the front door. When the occasion calls for a trip to the capital, to a restaurant or another hotel, a taxi's the best answer though you can hire a self-drive car in most places of the dune buggy variety, or you can cycle or moped around.

Island hopping can be done by air or boat. There is frequent inter-island air service in small planes; cruise liners call at a number of islands; and yachting fans make their own way.

# Eating and Drinking Solo

Not much fun but available. Obviously at its easiest for full board guests on some hideaway island. In the last decade, small restaurants have flourished at all the major resorts, sometimes run by ex-pats or born-and-bred islanders of British background. These days, too, there are familiar fast food outlets and plenty of beach bars.

Mostly everything has to be imported into the Caribbean so food is not wildly gourmet, and since currencies relate to the dollar, can work out expensive for what it is. At least the fruit is always good — papayas, mangos, bananas — and local vegetables like akee and cassava are staples. According to foodies, meals are best on the

French islands and the wine, cheaper. The cheapest alcohol is rum, always served liberally in party punches and best from Barbados and Jamaica. Jamaican coffee from the Blue Mountains is equally exceptional.

The Safety Factor

Not as good as it used to be which is why many Caribbean hotels have their own security guards. It may sound cowardly but a woman is best advised not to stay in a ground floor room in the major islands, and keep her door locked, or choose a tiny isle where the atmosphere is friendlier. That evening walk along the beach under the stars may not be such a good idea — rape and theft are the two most predominant crimes in major Caribbean resorts. For problems, call the general manager.

No-no's

Don't walk or drive in an open jeep alone at night is a general recommendation.
Don't visit local nightclubs by yourself unless you expect to be pestered.
Don't try doing the limbo if you have a bad back.
Don't select islands like the Grenadines if you can't stand your own company.

Essentials

Shops in island capitals like Bridgetown are well stocked with toilet requisites and in this island's case, British ones. Even on small islands, you'll find basic essentials. Luxury hotels have their own beauty salon. The electric current varies from island to island but is in the 110-220v range.

Medical Survival

To be on the safe side, stick to bottled water and take insect repellent with you. Regardless of what tourist board literature proclaims, mosquitoes do have the irritating habit of buzzing around the Caribbean and sand flies in some places do take a nip. Though sun creams are available, they are more costly than at home and are thoroughly necessary. Don't let a tan turn into a burn. All the better hotels will find you an English-speaking doctor if you need one.

What to do Solo

You don't need someone else around for the best of what there is to do in the Caribbean. Sunning, swimming and other watersports about sums it up. You can rent a small boat almost anywhere from a sunfish to something larger, join a glass-bottom boat trip, an island cruise. Skin diving is popular in many islands and water skiing on all. Which island has the best beach is a moot point — there are long, broad ones, small coves, white, black and gold sand ones. For its size, Antigua is said to have particularly fine ones and Barbados' west coast is another good bet.

Island highlights include a day out on the Jolly Roger in Barbados (rum by the gallon, lunch included and time for snorkelling); a raft trip in Jamaica; an outing to the bird sanctuary in Trinidad; an excursion to St Lucia's volcano.

Visas and Inoculations

Visas — none required
Inoculations — none compulsory, but typhoid and polio recommended.

Useful Addresses

Tourist Offices
Antigua Tourist Board, 15 Thayer Street, London W1. Tel: 01-486 7073
Antigua Department of Tourism, 610 Fifth Avenue, New York 10022. Tel: (212) 541 4117
Aruba Tourist Office, 1270 Sixth Avenue, New York, NY 10019. Tel: (212) 216 3030
Bahamas Ministry of Tourism, 23 Old Bond Street, London W1. Tel: 01-629 5238
Bahamas Tourist Office, 10 Columbus Circle, New York, NY 10023. Tel: (212) 757 1611
Barbados Board of Tourism, 6 Upper Belgrave Street, London SW1. Tel: 01-235 2449
Barbados Tourist Office, 800 Second Avenue, New York, NY 10017. Tel: (212) 986 6516
Eastern Caribbean Commission, 10 Kensington Court, London W8. Tel: 01-937 9522
Eastern Caribbean, 220 E 42nd Street, New York, NY 10017. Tel: (212) 986 9370
French West Indies Tourist Board, 610 Fifth Avenue, New York, NY 10022. Tel: (212) 757 1125
Jamaica Tourist Board, 50 St James's Street, London SW1. Tel: 01-493 3647
Jamaican Tourist Office, 2 Dag Hammarskjold Plaza, New York, NY

10017. Tel: (212) 688 7650

St Lucia Tourist Office, 41 E 42nd Street, New York, NY 10017. Tel: 867 2950

St Lucia Tourist Office, 1 Collingham Gardens, London SW5. Tel: 01-370 0926

Trinidad & Tobago Tourist Board, 20 Regent Street, London SW1. Tel: 01-839 7155

Trinidad Tourist Office, 400 Madison Avenue, New York, NY 10017. Tel: (212) 838 7750

British Virgin Islands Tourist Bureau, 48 Albemarle Street, London W1. Tel: 01-629 6353

British Virgin Islands Tourist Office, 370 Lexington Avenue, New York, NY 10016. Tel: (212) 696 0400

US Virgin Islands Tourist Office, 1270 Sixth Avenue, New York, NY 10019. Tel: (212) 582 4520

34 SOUTH AMERICA

Latin America is so vast and varied, one can only generalise about what to expect. Hygiene in many parts of these countries is not up to Western standards, for example, and plumbing often in disrepair. Bribery, theft, corruption are rampant — as much protection to person and property as possible should be taken. Cockroaches are just some of the 'crawlies' that are unpleasantly ubiquitous and English is absolutely useless off the beaten track (all of South America speaks Spanish or Portuguese). Health hazards are inevitable and practically no visitor escapes at least one bout with a stomach upset.

Travelling anywhere in South America (especially solo) is bound to meet with frustration. Officials are so document minded that it is probably wise to carry your passport with you at all times. Law enforcement works in nefarious ways. Establishing blame say in the case of an auto accident could take days; on the other hand a bribe could work effectively in a visitor's favour providing it is not an obvious bribe. Most Latin countries impose heavy penalties on drug users or carriers yet it is not unknown for the police to 'plant' drugs on innocent travellers.

So much for the bad things. On the plus side, South America can offer a wealth of travel experiences from ancient civilisations to majestic scenery, from cosmopolitan cities to fascinating customs and folklore. It is reasonable to feel that women are best off travelling in pairs, as couples or part of a group but that is not to say going it alone is is impossible. It has been done!

The Male Attitude

Given a ladylike demeanour and dress, a female visitor will find the majority of Latin Americans considerate and charming. Politeness is extended and expected in return (except perhaps when queueing). Because of cultural differences, a lone woman may come under a suspicious eye as one of ill repute (especially if hitchhiking) so that any problems which may arise are due to a genuine misunderstanding. Providing you are able to handle situations with panache you will be treated with the utmost courtesy.

A good number of Latin Americans are of European descent and over the years numerous Europeans have settled in this continent (e.g. Germans in Brazil), but much of the populace is also of Indian stock with a very different culture and way of life. Some, of mixed blood, may be known as *mestizos* or *mulattos* and some have a black heritage.

Where to Stay

Accommodation runs the gamut from the run down to the plush. The best hotels in capital cities can be very grand and elegant (also pricy in Rio or Buenos Aires). Boarding houses are abundant around bus and railway stations and markets under names like *casa de huéspedes, pensión, hospedaje, casa familiar* or *residencial*, but ask for recommendations. Remember that cheap hotels in poor areas have poor water supplies and subsequently bad sanitation.

Among the best hotels in Buenos Aires, Argentina are the Sheraton, Colón and the Crillon; the Plaza and Sheraton are excellent in La Pas, Bolivia; luxury properties in Santiago, Chile include the San Cristóbal Sheraton; Bogota, Colombia has a handsome Hilton and Quito, in Ecuador an Intercontinental. The Excelsior is reportedly the best in Asunción, Paraguay; Lima's Gran Bolivar and Crillón have long-standing reputations in Peru; Montevideo's (Uruguay) top hotels include the Internacional; Caracas, Venezuela the Tamanaco. In Brazil, Rio's Copacabana area, the Rio Othon Palace, Copacabana Palace and Meridien are among the finest; economy hotels are located in Flamengo/Botafogo, Lapa/Fátima and Saúde/Mauá districts. Tourists may also rent an apartment in Copacabana, Ipanema or Leblon.

Getting Around on Your Own

The road system in the continent has improved but there are still many roads which are unpaved. Train service is generally slow and unreliable. Long-distance bus service is best in Brazil, Chile and Venezuela but arrival times anywhere are unlikely to meet listed schedules.

In Argentina best travel bets are: the Visit Argentina Fare allows travel by air anywhere on Aerolineas Argentinas network for a fixed price during a 30 day period. (A tour must be planned in advance, however, as the voucher is exchanged for the appropriate set of tickets). An Argenpass is valid for a month's travel on Argentine railways and an Amerailpass allows Pullman travel for 16 days through several Latin American countries.

Few Brazilian cities are connected by rail but almost all are by road. Recommended routes are the sleeper train services between Rio and São Paulo or Belo Horizonte but you may be better off travelling by air. (Air passes issued by Varig, Vasp, Cruzeiro and Transbrasil are economical, but must be purchased outside Brazil).

Making reservations for transport in Chile can be difficult though buses are numerous and trains not as slow as in other Andean countries. Lan-Chile and Ledeco offer a Visit Chile air pass for purchase abroad.

Unlimited domestic air travel for 30 days is possible in Colombia with the aid of an Avianca pass puchased abroad. Ask about shared taxi and microbus services rather than regular long-distance bus travel.

Few Peruvian roads are paved apart from the Pan-American and Central Highways. Bus travel is uncomfortable but *colectivos* go almost everywhere (bookings should be made at least a day in advance). These are also the ideal mode of transport for getting around Venezuela although good bus service operates between major cities.

Eating and Drinking Solo

In Buenos Aires look for tea rooms which can be pleasant places to be alone in. The intellectual cognoscenti use the bars and coffee shops on Avenida Corrientes and on Lavalle you will see a number of suitable *whiskerias* or *cervecerias* which serve either coffee or exotic cocktails. A *confiteria* is a tea room cum cocktail lounge.

Not surprisingly, beef is first class in Argentina and many dishes are based on it like *bife a caballo* (steak topped by a fried egg) or an *asado* (roast). *Carbonadas* of minced beef and *churrascos* (thick grilled steaks are all excellent). Argentine wines are pleasant enough and far less expensive than other alcohol.

In La Paz international food is expensive — restaurants serving this more familiar fare are concentrated on Av. 16 de Julio (the Prado), Av. 6 de Agosto and Av. 20 de Octubre. In the shopping and business district you'll find many cheap restaurants serving local spicy Bolivian food, but also snack bars. Don't eat from food stalls or markets. A typical Bolivian speciality is a *sulténa* (meat stew in pastry) often made with red chillies. The local hot maize drink is *api* but *singani* is rather ferocious.

In Rio which is possibly the most Europeanised place of all, there's no shortage of hamburger stands where you can safely eat. *Galetos* lunch counters are very reasonable for grilled meats as are the *churrascarias*. Tea rooms are very fashionable and sedate enough but note that a respectable nightclub will not allow you entrance by yourself! The young set rendezvous at any of the pavement cafés along the resort areas and *gafieras* (restaurants or night clubs with live Brazilian music) are 'in' right now.

Usual Brazilian dishes are beef or chicken with rice and black beans — the most famous dish with beans is the *feijoada*. Exotic fruits always available include mangos, jackfruit, custard apples and guava, and are often added to make zesty ice creams. Fruit juice is readily for sale, local wines are okay, but imported liquor is very expensive and the local firewater, *cachaca*, a killer.

In Santiago, good hamburgers and ice cream are featured by many snack places on Ahumada. A number of bars serve light food — popular ones are located on Pedro Valdivia. The Chilean capital also boasts tea rooms and fast food outlets, plus expresso bars.

The most typical dish is *cazeuela de ave*, a kind of chicken stew whilst an *empanada frita* (fried meat pasty) is perfect between meals. Interesting seafood might tempt you to an abalone starter or a conger stew. Chilean wines are particularly good — look for those from the central areas — the best are marked *vino reservado*. And don't forget to try a pisco sour.

In Bogota, the best street for pavement cafés and bars is Carrera 15 and women alone will be fine in the Colombian capital's tea rooms (a chain of good pastry shops is Cyranos). The meal speciality in Bogota is belly of beef but regular grilled meats are always listed on menus. Local wines and beer are both acceptable.

In Lima, the Rimac section of the city is good for cheap food, e.g. chicken restaurants on Av. Trujillo, those on Av. Venezuela and the snack bars on Unión. Don't be surprised to see 'Kentucky Fried Chicken' or 'Pizza Hut' signs — they're here. The best local Peruvian fare is to be found in the taverns (*chicherias*) and the small restaurants called *picanterias*. Much of the food is highly spiced and no one should miss sampling *ceviche*, marinated and spiced raw fish. Any dish described as *arequipeño* is expectedly hot and spicy. Good reasonable food is to be found in *chifas* (Chinese restaurants). Beer and local wines are fair.

Residents of Montevideo appear to eat later than elsewhere in Latin America. Tea shops in town are known as *confiterias* — popular ones are located along 18 de Julio. The Uruguayan capital also boasts a large number of *heladerias* (ice cream parlours) and *coctelerias* (cocktail lounges) which also serve myriad hors d'oeuvres. There are lots of *parrilladas* serving grilled meat; *chivite* is a popular beef snack. Local wines tend to vary in quality but beers are good.

In Caracas, budgeteers should look for *fuentes de soda* and cafés. A good selection of restaurants can be found around Av. Urdaneta, but you may not feel comfortable in a *cerveceria*. Venezuelan beef is comparable with Argentina's and local fish like pargo is A1. The most popular snack is a toasted *arepa* (sandwich); most common beers, Polar and Zulia but no local wines. Bottled water in cheap restaurants often comes from the tap.

 **The Safety Factor**

I can't say that Latin America as a whole is particularly safe most especially when it comes to theft and pickpocketing. You should never accept anything to eat, drink or smoke from any fellow passenger on public transport — it could be drugged. It is also advisable to take taxis between airport and hotel. Try not to look too much like a tourist, don't wear expensive jewellery and don't carry your money all in one place. It would be equally foolish to wander in isolated places or walk down narrow city streets alone at night. In an emergency call the Embassy.

Rio has become notorious for its rise in crime, unfortunately as bad on its famous beaches as it is in its streets at night, so be wary of gangs of small boys and don't walk alone after dark — don't expect help from the police. The most dangerous areas to avoid are Dois Immãos, Santa Teresa, Copacabana's Av. Atlantica, Pão de Açucar, Corcovado, Quinta da Boa Vista, Jardim Botanico, Joquei Clube racecourse area and around the Hotel Intercontinental at São Conrado. On a Sunday, the police are so busy trying to guard the beaches that the city centre is not well policed.

No-no's

Wear shorts only on the beach or for sports — they are frowned upon throughout Latin America.
Don't roll your own cigarettes — you may be suspected of carrying drugs and be subjected to intensive searching.
Be careful of exchanging money on the black market — there can be plain clothes police raids.
If you do hitchhike, don't accept a lift from a car with two people in it.
Be especially wary in Bogota of anyone describing himself as a plain clothes policeman — the old part of town around Plaza Bolivar and from Calle 28 are the most potentially dangerous for assault.
Don't hitchhike at all in Paraguay.

Essentials

In the major city shops, all necessities are sold. If touring, take toilet paper with you — toilets are often without it. Bring as much film as you can — it's expensive to buy.
Leather is a good buy in Argentina; llama and alpaca goods in Bolivia; jewellery in Brazil; emeralds in Colombia.

Electricity: Buenos Aires 220v, 50 cycles; Rio 110-220v, 60 cycles; Santiago 220v, 50 cycles; Bogota 120v, DC; Quito 110v, 60 cycles; Lima 220v, 60 cycles; Montevideo 220v, 50 cycles; Caracas 110v, 60 cycles.

Medical Survival

The general rule for South America is don't drink the water, steer clear of ice, watch salads and fruit that can't be peeled. Before you travel recommended inoculations are yellow fever, typhoid, tetanus and polio. Remember hepatitis is endemic throughout the continent and malaria is another potential problem. You may also suffer from high altitude sickness or too much heat if you over exert yourself.

When you order bottled water, ensure it is opened in your presence and don't risk buying food (hot or cold) from wayside stalls. Water sterilizing tablets are available in some of the city chemists but go prepared with them; likewise, anti-malarial pills. English-speaking doctors are available in the major cities, and hospitals provide first aid service. Make sure you have sufficient medical insurance before you travel.

What to do Solo

One of the most impressive public buildings in Argentina's *Buenos Aires* is the Teatro Colón, a great opera house, very red plush and gilt; of the many churches, San Ignacio de Loyola is the city's oldest colonial building. As always a city organised tour helps to get your bearings. At its heart is Plaza de Mayo (looked upon by the Casa Rosada); north of this square you'll find this shopping, theatre and commercial district. Calle Florida here (for shops) is pedestrianised in the afternoon so it's a great rendezvous spot. A less expensive shopping street is Avenida Santa Fe. Good restaurants and cafés are located on Avenida Corrientes, pedestrianised Calle Lavalle and other nearby streets.

One of the city's broad avenues, Paseo Colon, leads to the colourful port district, the Boca, whose houses are splashed with bright hues, and cobbled streets wind between them. This is where Buenos Aires was founded; today an Italian district. On a hot day a walk along Avenida Costanera by the riverfront may be an idea — there is outdoor dining and concerts in the gardens.

Artists' quarter is the Barrio centred on Calle Independencia; Sunday antique markets are held at the Plaza Dorrego. (Watch out for pickpockets here and at all the other weekend markets).

The capital's summer bathing resorts are Mar del Plata and Miramar but they're both a good distance away. Indeed, the country itself is vast and split into regions of great contrasts, ranging from cattle ranches to mountains. One of the country's natural highlights (shared with Brazil) is Iguazu Falls, higher and wider than Niagara. The very furthest south you can go is the island of Tierra del Fuego.

La Paz, Bolivia's capital is the world's highest — ask for *mate de coca* to relieve altitude sickness. Much of the city is modern, around Plaza Murillo — the main shopping street is Calle Comercio (though the raucous atmosphere of the Mercado Camacho on Av. Camacho has the photographic appeal with Indian vendors in their hard-brimmed bowler hats). Try and see an Indian wedding at San Francisco Church on a Saturday morning or look for handicrafts in the rows of small shops on Calle Sagárnaga which runs from Plaza San Francisco. One of the liveliest streets in the Indian quarter is Avenida Buenos Aires.

One of this country's natural highlights is Lake Titicaca (shared with Peru) where the town of Copacabana is the base. From here it is possible to hire boats to visit the lake's islands with their Inca monuments.

Tough Brasilia is the capital of Brazil, most visitors want to see *Rio de Janeiro*, whose February Carnival has to be one of the world's most famous events. Although there is plenty to see in the city itself, it is the resort suburbs which are the draw. Most densely populated of all is Copacabana, a narrow strip between mountains and sea with fashionable shops along Avenida Copacabana and Rua Barata Riveiro (many with familiar names) plus a mass of skyscrapers.

Only slightly less crowded are the seaside resorts of Ipanema and Leblon. Overlooking it all are the two great landmarks: Corcovado and Sugar Loaf Mountain (visits are best made in a group). Corcovado is the peak on which stands the huge statue of Christ — a cog train runs to its base; the huge cone of Sugar Loaf is reached via cable car. From both the vista, when not obscured by mist, is unforgettable. Rio's summer capital is Petropolis, high in the hills.

One of the most interesting regions of Brazil is Bahia, still very rich in folklore. In Salvador, the provincial capital, the stall vendors are usually black women (Bahianas) dressed in eighteenth-century costume whilst the *capoeira* (a traditional dance) was developed from the foot fighting technique introduced by African slaves. You might also see a *candomble*, the magical-mystical partly religious ceremony which also derived from Africa.

Organised Amazon trips are an adventurous alternative, and are featured by British tour operators.

The centre of *Santiago* extends between the Mapocho and Avenida O'Higgins with Plaza de Armas its hub, bordered by arcaded shops, the Cathedral and archbishop's palace. The best view of the city is from Santa Lucia Hill, crowned by a colonial fortress (the Hidalgo Castle) with its noon-day guns. Santiago's oldest church is located between Calle San Francisco and Calle Londres, next to the Museum of Colonial Art. In Parque O'Higgins (he was a general) there is an amusement park, recreational facilities and restaurants, plus an open air stage where local songs and dances are performed. Since ballet is so popular in Santiago a number of free performances are given in summer in the city parks. The arty will find the neighbourhood of Lastarria interesting for its studios, theatres and antique shops. One of the big art fairs takes place in November in Parque Forestal; also in autumn one of the most colourful flower shows in Parque Cerrillos.

Main shopping area is Paseo Ahumada and Paseo Huérfanos, both pedestrianised streets.

One of Chile's great ski centres is not far from the capital — Portillo. Several high society resorts are close to Valparaiso (main Chilean port), like Viña del Mar.

Bogota's altitude may make some people dizzy especially those headed immediately for the top of Monserrate, reached by funicular, for an overall view. At the heart of the Colombian capital is Plaza Bolivar surrounded by the old quarter (Barrio La Candelaria). The remains of Bogota's colonial past are to be seen in this district: massive mansions, the Palace of San Carlos, the Municipal Palace, the Churches of San Ignacio, Santa Clara, San Agustin. One of the very best of many museums is Museo del Oro at the Parque de Santander — its collection of precolumbian gold work is unique.

One of Colombia's most interesting towns is Cartagena for its old walled town; the most popular seaside resort, Santa Marta.

Quito is extremely close to the Equator but high enough not to roast. Its charm lies in its cobbled colonial centre with Plaza

Independencia its middle and the best way to see it is on foot. One of the district's oldest streets is Calle Morales in the Lan Ronda area but the main shopping district is Carrera Guayaquil. Although street trading has officially ceased it still carries on in practice with daily markets held from Sucreo 24 de Mayo and from San Francisco Church to past Cuenca. There are numerous museums in Quito and 86 churches of which La Compañia is probably the most ornate.

Overlooking Quito is the peak of Cruz Loma (a favourite with hikers) but don't climb it alone except by taxi. Another excursion is to the Equatorial Line Monument but make sure you have warm clothing with you.

Although it is a seaport, Guayaquil is a pleasant stop in Ecuador and livelier than the capital. West of the Ecuadorean coast, the Galápagos Islands are renowned for their wildlife — several British tour operators feature tours here.

Paraguay's only major city is its capital, *Asunción*, whose three busiest streets are Estrella, Oliva, Palma and whose prettiest parks are Parque Carlos Antonio López (for its view); Parque Caballero (with waterfalls); and Parque Gaspar Rodriguez de Francia. The botanical gardens lie along the Paraguay River.

Lima spans both sides of the Rio Rimac at the base of Cerro San Cristóbal. Most sights of touristic interest are around Plaza de Armas; the newer section of the city centres on Plaza San Martin. The main (pedestrianised) shopping street is Jirón de la Unión; on this street also is the entrance to the Palacio de Gobierno. Lima's cathedral is on Plaza de Armas itself, richly silvered and said to contain Pizarro's remains. City sightseeing tours will take you to major monuments, churches, museums and parks and on short excursions to the handsome suburb of Miraflores and the bathing resorts of Chorrillos and La Herradura.

Of the many possibilities in Peru, the priority trip is to Cuzco and from there to Machu Picchu. This requires overnighting in the little town of Cuzco and a full day's train excursion to the Inca ruins which for years were buried in jungle growth until Hiram Bingham rediscovered them in 1911 (a guided tour is necessary). A side trip can also be taken to Pisac market — marvellous for photography although it has become expensive and is overrun with tourists.

Plaza Independencia is *Montevideo*'s centre around which the Uruguayan capital's life revolves; the old town is a little way away — a number of small squares cut into the busy Avenida 18 de Julio. The residential areas are also seaside resorts of which Pocitos has the best facilities, but one of the major sport and beach resorts is Punta del Este, a good distance away.

Caracas' official centre is Plaza Bolivar but since it has grown, there are several 'centres' including Plaza Venezuela, Sabana Grande, Chacaito, La Floresta and Boleita. Parks, museums and the two national monuments can be seen on guided tours and, whilst Caracas is a lively late-hours city, women are not recommended to walk the streets alone at night. There are several beaches on the city's doorstep and Caracas is frequently a port of call on Caribbean cruise itineraries.

Visas and Inoculations

Visas — none required, but requirements do change; double check.
Inoculations — none compulsory, but cholera, malaria pills, typhoid, polio and yellow fever recommended.

Useful Addresses

Embassies
British Embassy, Luis Agote 2412/52, Buenos Aires, Argentina. Tel: 80 7071
British Hospital, Calle Perdriel 74, Buenos Aires, Argentina. Tel: 23 1081
British Embassy, Av. Arce 2732-2734, La Paz, Bolivia. Tel: 351 400
British Consulate, Praia do Flamengo 284, Rio, Brazil. Tel: 225 7252
British Embassy, La Concepcion 177, 4th floor, Providencia 1800, Santiago, Chile. Tel: 2239 166
British Embassy, Calle 38 No. 13-37, Bogota, Colombia. Tel: 287 81 00
British Embassy, Av. González Suárez 111, Quito, Ecuador. Tel: 230 070
British Embassy, Presidente Franco 706, Esquina O'Leary, Asunción, Paraguay. Tel: 49146
British Embassy, Edificio Pacifico-Washington, Plaza Washington, Lima, Peru. Tel: 283830
British Embassy, Marco Bruto 1073, Montevideo, Uruguay. Tel: 780352
The English Club, Treinta y Tres, Montevideo, Uruguay. Tel: 82180
The British Hospital, Av. Italia 2420, Montevideo, Uruguay. Tel: 409011
British Embassy, Torre Las Mercedes, Cuidad Comercial Tamanco, Chuao, Caracas, Venezuela. Tel: 911255
US Embassy, Avenida Colombia 4300, Buenos Aires, Argentina. Tel: 774 7611
US Embassy, Edificio Banco Popular, Calle Colon 290, La Paz, Bolivia. Tel: 350251
US Embassy, Avenida Presidente Wilson 147, Rio, Brazil. Tel: 292 7117
US Embassy, Agustines 1343, Santiago, Chile. Tel: 710133
US Embassy, Calle 38 No. 8-61, Bogota, Colombia. Tel: 285 1300
US Embassy, Avenida Patria 120, Quito, Ecuador. Tel: 548 000
US Embassy, Avenida Mariscal Lopez and Kubitschek, Asunción, Paraguay. Tel: 201041
US Embassy, Garcilaso de la Vega 1400, Lima, Peru. Tel: 286000
US Embassy, Rambia Wilson 1776, Montevideo, Uruguay. Tel: 409051
US Embassy, Avenida Francisco Miranda, La Floresta, Caracas, Venezuela. Tel: 284 6111

Tourist Offices

Argentine Embassy, 111 Cadogan Gardens, London SW3. Tel: 01-730 4388
National Tourist Office, Santa Fe 883, Buenos Aires, Argentina. Tel: 31 2300
Bolivia Embassy, 106 Eaton Square, London SW1. Tel: 01-235 4248
National Tourist Office, Edif. Hermann, Banco de Boston Bld, Plaza Venezuela, La Paz, Bolivia. Tel: 367 463
Brazilian Embassy, 32 Green Street, London W1. Tel: 01-493 0565
Brazilian Tourist Association, 60 E 42nd Street, New York, NY 10017. Tel: (212) 286 9600
Tourist Information, Sala do Turismo, Praça Mauá 7, Embratur, Rua Mariz e Barros 13, Rio, Brazil. Tel: 273 2177
Chilean Embassy, 12 Devonshire Street, London W1. Tel: 01-580 6392
National Tourist Office, Sernatur, Catedral 1165, Casilla 14082, Santiago, Chile. Tel: 82151
Colombian Embassy, 3 Hans Crescent, London SW1. Tel: 01-589 9177
Tourist Office, Calle 28 No. 13A-15, Bogota, Colombia. Tel: 283 9466
Ecuadorian Embassy, 3 Hans Crescent, London SW1. Tel: 01-584 1367
Tourist Office, Reina Victoria 514 y Roca, Quito, Ecuador. Tel: 239 044
Paraguay Embassy, Braemar Lodge, Cornwall Gardens, London SW7. Tel: 01-937 1253
Peruvian Embassy, 52 Sloane Street, London SW1. Tel: 01-235 1917
Tourist Office, Enturperu, Av. Javier Prado-Oeste 1358, San Isidro, Lima, Peru. Tel: 419753
Consulate of Uruguay, 48 Lennox Gardens, London SW1. Tel: 01-589 8735
Venezuelan Embassy, 1 Cromwell Road, London SW7. Tel: 01-581 2776

INDEX

Europe 1-88
  Belgium 3-7
    accommodation 3
    attitude 3
    eating/drinking 4
    essentials 5
    safety 5
    sightseeing 5-6
    transport 4
    useful addresses 7
  France 8-14
    accommodation 9
    attitude 8
    eating/drinking 10
    essentials 11
    safety 11
    sightseeing 12-13
    transport 9
    useful addresses 13
  Greece 15-19
    accommodation 16
    attitude 15
    eating/drinking 16
    essentials 17
    safety 17
    sightseeing 18
    transport 16
    useful addresses 19
  Holland 20-5
    accommodation 21
    attitude 20
    eating/drinking 22
    essentials 23
    safety 23
    sightseeing 24
    transport 21
    useful addresses 25
  Hungary 26-9
    accommodation 26
    attitude 26
    eating/drinking 27
    essentials 28
    safety 27
    sightseeing 28
    transport 27
    useful addresses 29
  Italy 30-5
    accommodation 31
    attitude 30
    eating/drinking 32
    essentials 33
    safety 33
    sightseeing 34
    transport 31
    useful addresses 35
  Malta 36-9
    accommodation 36
    attitude 36
    eating/drinking 37
    essentials 37
    safety 37
    sightseeing 38
    transport 37
    useful addresses 39
  Portugal 40-3
    accommodation 40
    attitude 40
    eating/drinking 41
    essentials 42
    safety 42
    sightseeing 42
    transport 41
    useful addresses 43
  Romania 44-7
    accommodation 44
    attitude 44
    eating/drinking 45
    essentials 46
    safety 45
    sightseeing 46
    transport 45
    useful addresses 47
  Scandinavia 48-53
    accommodation 49
    attitude 48
    eating/drinking 50
    essentials 50
    safety 50
    sightseeing 51-2
    transport 49
    useful addresses 52
  The Socialist Bloc 54-7
    accommodation 55
    attitude 55
    eating/drinking 55
    essentials 56
    sightseeing 56
    transport 55
    useful addresses 57
  Spain 58-62
    accommodation 59
    attitude 58
    eating/drinking 59
    essentials 60
    safety 60
    sightseeing 61-2
    transport 59
    useful addresses 62
  Switzerland 63-6
    accommodation 63
    attitude 63
    eating/drinking 64
    essentials 65

INDEX

safety 64
sightseeing 65-6
transport 64
useful addresses 66
Turkey 67-71
  accommodation 68
  attitude 67
  eating/drinking 68
  essentials 69
  safety 69
  sightseeing 70
  transport 68
  useful addresses 71
UK 72-7
  accommodation 73
  attitude 72
  eating/drinking 74
  essentials 75
  safety 75
  sightseeing 76
  transport 73
  useful addresses 77
West Germany & Austria 78-83
  accommodation 79
  attitude 78
  eating/drinking 80
  essentials 81
  safety 81
  sightseeing 82
  transport 79
  useful addresses 83
Yugoslavia 84-8
  accommodation 85
  attitude 84
  eating/drinking 86
  essentials 87
  safety 86
  sightseeing 87
  transport 85
  useful addresses 88
The Middle East 89-105
Cyprus 91-3
  accommodation 92
  attitude 91
  eating/drinking 92
  essentials 92
  safety 92
  sightseeing 93
  transport 92
  useful addresses 93
Egypt 94-9
  accommodation 95
  attitude 94
  eating/drinking 96
  essentials 97
  safety 96
  sightseeing 97-8
  transport 95
  useful addresses 99
Israel 100-5
  accommodation 101
  attitude 100
  eating/drinking 101
  essentials 102
  safety 102
  sightseeing 103-4
  transport 101
  useful addresses 105
Africa 107-17
Morocco & Tunisia 109-13
  accommodation 110
  attitude 109
  eating/drinking 110
  essentials 111
  safety 111
  sightseeing 112
  transport 110
  useful addresses 113
Kenya 114-17
  accommodation 115
  attitude 114
  eating/drinking 115
  essentials 116
  safety 115
  sightseeing 116
  transport 115
  useful addresses 117
Asia and The Far East 119-58
India 121-6
  accommodation 122
  attitude 121
  eating/drinking 123
  essentials 125
  safety 124
  sightseeing 125-6
  transport 122
  useful addresses 126
Japan 127-32
  accommodation 128
  attitude 127
  eating/drinking 129
  essentials 130
  safety 129
  sightseeing 130-1
  transport 128
  useful addresses 132
China 133-8
  accommodation 134
  attitude 133
  eating/drinking 135
  essentials 136
  safety 136
  sightseeing 137
  transport 134
  useful addresses 138
Thailand 139-43
  accommodation 140
  attitude 139
  eating/drinking 141
  essentials 141
  safety 141
  sightseeing 142
  transport 140
  useful addresses 143
Malaysia 144-7
  accommodation 144
  attitude 144
  eating/drinking 145
  essentials 146
  safety 145
  sightseeing 146
  transport 145
  useful addresses 147
Indonesia 148-52
  accommodation 149
  attitude 148
  eating/drinking 149
  essentials 150
  safety 150

sightseeing 150
transport 149
useful addresses
  152
Australia & New
  Zealand 153-8
  accommodation
    154
  attitude 153
  eating/drinking
    155
  essentials 156
  safety 155
  sightseeing 156-7
  transport 154
  useful addresses
    158
The Americas 159-91
  Canada 161-5
    accommodation
      162
    attitude 161
    eating/drinking
      163
    essentials 164
    safety 163
    sightseeing 164
    transport 162
    useful addresses
      165
  USA 166-71
    accommodation
      167
    attitude 166
    eating/drinking
      169
    essentials 170
    safety 169
    sightseeing 170
    transport 168
    useful addresses
      171
  Mexico 172-6
    accommodation
      172
    attitude 172
    eating/drinking
      173
    essentials 174
    safety 174
    sightseeing 175
    transport 173
    useful addresses
      176
  Caribbean 177-81
    accommodation
      178
    attitude 177
    eating/drinking
      178
    essentials 179
    safety 179
    sightseeing 180
    transport 178
    useful addresses
      180
  South America 182-91
    accommodation
      183
    attitude 182
    eating/drinking
      184
    essentials 186
    safety 185
    sightseeing 187-9
    transport 183
    useful addresses
      190